Walk!

Lanzarote

with

David & Ros Brawn

DISCOVERY WALKING GUIDES LTD

Walk! Lanzarote
First Edition - June 2004
Second Edition - July 2009
Third Edition - August 2012

Copyright © 2012

Published by
Discovery Walking Guides Ltd
10 Tennyson Close, Northampton NN5 7HJ,
England

Maps
Maps are adapted from Lanzarote Tour & Trail Map
published by **Discovery Walking Guides Ltd**

Photographs
All photographs in this book were taken by the
authors, Ros & David Brawn.

Front Cover Photographs

La Geria   PR LZ waypost

Haria   Los Cocoteros to Costa Teguise

ISBN 9781904946830

Text and photographs* © David & Ros Brawn

Walk! Lanzarote
CONTENTS

WHAT'S NEW?

We went to the Fire Island in Feb 2012 with a list of walking 'want to do's'. Well, as John Lennon famously said, "Life is what happens to you while you're busy making other plans." and so it was to prove for us.

What Worked (as compared to what we had planned)

First on our list was an ascent up **Montaña Negra** (515m) sitting across the LZ56 from **Montaña Cuervo**; the trail curving up the eastern face of the cone is clearly visible from the road. A specific reason for tackling this ascent was to get the view and photos - not only into **Montaña Cuervo** from above, but also elevated views across the volcanic cones and lava sea. It's an exposed climb best tackled in calm conditions, which we didn't get; Lanzarote is windy, as it proves, each time we visit.

We also hoped to get a circular route in this region around the volcanic cones, possibly including some ascents, but the volcanic grit underfoot means a lot of hard walking for very little reward amongst the shifting trails, winds rearranging the loose *picon*, making any planned route effectively 'off path' navigation, requiring GPS for any degree of accuracy.

Frustrated by windy weather, we drove up the LZ56 to the large parking area between **Montañas Tiguaton** and **Cortijo** where we discovered an easy strolling dirt track heading SW and S to the base of **Montaña Los Rodeos**. At the foot of the cone we opted to go anticlockwise around the cone, where after a brief climb we come to a saddle between the **Rodeos** and **Rilla** cones, from where a rough jeep track leads straight up to the 454 metre summit of **Los Rodeos**, an option for the route if you're up for the climb and it's not too windy. From this point we have a superb view (E & NE) over a green lava river, frozen in time - before continuing around the cone to meet our inward route. For much of this route we are 'nose to nose' with the impenetrable lava sea while all the walking is on a well-stabilised dirt track, making this a suitable route for an 'all the family' outing.

We considered reducing/consolidating our coastal promenade routes but people asked us to keep them in, as they are easy strolling routes for all the family. On arriving in **Costa Teguise**, we found that our Walk 3 had not only been officially adopted, but also extended into the local countryside to produce a 10km route with two shorter alternatives. It was also pleasing to renew acquaintance with **Helga's Kitchen** for excellent coffee and cakes, tucked away from tourist eyes, yet in the centre of the resort.

There's just something about walking along a rugged coastline above waves crashing against the rocks below, with options for bathing along the way. These routes are more rugged on the ground than they look on the map and so it proved with our new **Los Cocoteros - Costa Teguise** coastal route. It's a linear route, though why not plan a day's hiking? Walk into **Costa Teguise**, refreshments (**Helga's Kitchen**?) and an afternoon return to **Los Cocoteros**.

Lots of people asked for a coastal route across the Hidden Barrancos to make a linear route between **Puerto del Carmen** and **Playa Blanca**. We didn't get to record this ourselves; we pieced together other people's GPS records into a reliable route that picks up our Walk 18 **Femés** to **Playa Blanca** at around 200 metres altitude; higher than we'd been hoping for but much better than ascending all the way to the ridge overlooking **Femés**.

Just once in a while a new route will drop into our lap. Which is what happened with our new **Yaiza - Las Breñas - Yaiza** circular route, that came about from looking at other people's GPS tracks which showed a possible walking trail out of **La Degollada** (SW to S) and another possible trail out of **Las Breñas** across the *malpais* (NNE) circling **Montaña Cinta** back to **Yaiza**.

It worked out beautifully on the ground. **Las Breñas** now boasts two restaurants (both closed Mondays), including our favourite **Casa Marcos**, making this a unique opportunity to include great walking with art (Dieter Noss' house) and great refreshments at halfway. The route has been 'trail tested' and approved by a couple of our DWG eNews subscribers, and is surprisingly unknown to the authorities who installed the myriad of wayposts that now dot the island.

We couldn't claim **La Geria** as a new route, but we now have a circular option returning to **Yaiza** across the *malpais* below **Montaña Tinasoria** on a series of dirt tracks. We've also added a different finish option to the main **La Geria** walk, following the new wayposts plus the additional directions that you'll need for a finish in the centre of **Puerto del Carmen** or at the large roundabout at the western end of the resort.

Across the island a host of official PR (*Pequeño Recorrido* - short day route) Wayposts have been installed. We've seen a comment online saying that there's no need for a guide book because you can use the wayposts; well, you *could* but mostly you would soon be lost.

The network of paths consists of ten routes; 01 **Arrieta** to **Caleta de Famara**, 03 **Teguise** to **Caleta de Famara**, 04 **Teguise** to **Guatiza**, 05 **Tiagua** to **Caleta de Famara**, 06 **Mozaga** to **Yaiza**, 09 **Femés** to **Playa Blanca** (DWG route), 11 **Femés** to **Playa Quemada** (DWG route), 16 **Haría** to **Ermita de las Nieves** (DWG route), 19 **Mancha Blanca** to **Playa de las Malvas**, 20 **Caleta de Famara** to **Tinajo**. There are information boards at the start and finish of each route giving brief directions and a map - *not* a Tour & Trail Map.

The wayposts are useful if you know how to use them but on their own they are more likely to produce confusion as in our new circular route based on **Tabayesco**. Normally we avoid 'open ground' walking routes but having an interesting suggestion for a circular route based on **Tabayesco**, we realised that this suggestion would give us the potential for circular routes as an alternative to our long linear routes from **Mala** and **Haría** to **Teguise** we decided to see the route on the ground. It is a good example of where the new wayposts confuse rather than help as we encounter an isolated waypost below **Peña de la Pequeña** shortly after which all traces of a route disappear! There are plenty of wrong options you could take, so best to follow our directions for the pathless descent or ascent from **Tabayesco**. This new route can be combined, mixed and matched, with our other routes to give you a range of walking route options.

Lanzarote Tour & Trail Super-Durable Map 3rd edition (pub. 2012)

One big change following on from our Costa Blanca Mountains Super-Durable Map is our new method of producing the terrain model of contours for T&T maps, allowing us to produce 20 metre contours more quickly than we used to produce 50 metre contours. The system is not perfect however, as the NASA survey data tends to 'fall apart' when it encounters steep terrain, meaning that it got totally confused by the **Famara** cliffs, requiring David spending a lot of time correcting the data.

Despite this frailty, it will mean that all new T&T maps will incorporate 20 metre contours, giving a much better definition of the landscape than was possible with our earlier 50 metre contour model.

As usual we've been busy GPS recording the new roads (not so many) and roundabouts (more of these) to produce the new road layouts which combined with our new walking research result in our new 3rd edition Lanzarote Tour & Trail Super-Durable Map.

THE AUTHORS

David and Ros Brawn moved to southern Tenerife in the spring of 1988. Finding a large resort filled with 'lost' tourists their first project was to produce the first integrated street plan of Las Americas/Los Cristianos whose current editions continue to provide the resort mapping that everyone uses - see 'Geranium Walk'. Discovering the resort hinterland resulted in the first 'Warm Island Walking Guide' for Tenerife South closely followed by guides for the North and West, then La Gomera and so Discovery Walking Guides was born.

Over two decades later, David & Ros have hundreds of books and maps to their credit and despite having to split their time between the DWG office (UK) DWG research (mostly Spain and its islands) and Australia's Sunshine Coast Hinterland (Maleny) they still think of Tenerife as their 'Home' island.

Having pioneered the use of GPS for walkers, they've surveyed and mapped to produce the 'Tour & Trail' series of maps used to illustrate Walk! guide books and the popular 'Bus & Touring' maps. Along the way David became a member of the British Cartographic Society including contributions to its Maplines magazine.

For a full list of destinations covered by David and Ros see:
www.walking.demon.co.uk   www.dwgwalking.co.uk

HISTORY

Lanzarote and Fuerteventura's first inhabitants were the *Majos* (or Mahos), the approximate equivalent of the *Guanches* in the western Canary Islands. It is thought that they led a relatively uneventful existence until 1402, when the Norman *conquistador* Jean de Bethencourt arrived, befriending the *Majo* leader and taking peaceful control of the island from a camp in **Rubicón**, soon passing power to his nephew Maciot, the founder of the island's original capital **Teguise**.

.. 'coloured hills' as seen from the west coast ..

The *Majos* named the island 'Titerroygatra', which translates as 'coloured hills', a name which would be just as appropriate today, though its current name is an adaptation of the name of an influential immigrant, Lancelotto Malocello.

GEOGRAPHY

Lanzarote is the most northerly and least mountainous of the Canary Islands, its highest point being 675 metres, **Peñas del Chache**, unfortunately taken over by the military and off limits to walkers. Its 169 kilometres of coastline varies between yellow and black beaches, cliffs and lava *malpaís*, offering some photogenic scenes. The island has been repeatedly shaped by volcanic activity, the most famous being the 1730-36 eruptions which formed **Timanfaya**, and the last in 1824 which created the volcanoes of **Tinguatón**, **Tao** and **Nuevo del Fuego**.

CLIMATE & AGRICULTURE

Lanzarote's close proximity to Africa is apparent in its weather. The dry, desert-like climate is interrupted by a few rainy days, typically in winter and early spring, but not amounting to much; for this reason the island's water supply comes from desalination plants. The modest height of Lanzarote's hills is insufficient to benefit from the humidity of the trade winds, but even so the lack of rain has not deterred the islanders from devising methods of growing a wide range of fruits and vegetables.

Particularly remarkable are the *zocos*, notably in **La Geria** where the black volcanic *picón* (ash) filters moisture to the roots and mulches the soil beneath, while keeping the plants cool. This is a windy island, and the agricultural plots are often protected from the prevailing winds by horseshoe shaped walls. When easterly winds blow they bring hot, dust-laden *calimas*, best avoided by staying indoors.

Ring 'o Roses

Lanzarote continues to display new 'thingies'. On our latest research trip we snapped a few new ones for your amusement (and ours). However, this time we're not telling where we found them - it should be fun for you to notice them on your travels around the island. See our website for the details of each thingy's location.

1. Inanimate object that the speaker has temporarily forgotten the name of.
2. Large, or over large, man-made object of no discernible use prominently displayed in a public place, notably in the centre of large roundabouts. Associated with the Canary Island of Lanzarote and its most famous citizen César Manrique (artist, 1919-1992).

César Manrique's legacy to Lanzarote is apparent in many aspects of the island's life, visibly in the squat white painted houses with green or blue window

Dr Who Monster Thingy

Large Thingy in several parts

shutters but most notably in the 'sculptures' adorning roundabouts on the island's main roads.

Sailing Thingy

Whether you consider these constructions as art seems open to question. Is the huge green tin-can cactus, outside the gardens in **Guatiza**, art or simply an advertisement in the same genre that American and Australian businesses use, equivalent to a giant 'hamburger' outside a burger bar?

Some residents are defensive over these

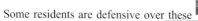

Curvy Thingy

Thingys, believing that anything César Manrique promoted must be good for the island. You'll have plenty of opportunities to form your own Thingy opinion as you travel round.

Giant Key

Skinny Thingy

Egg Whisk and Planet

Nude Unicyling Thingy

When our 'Thingy' comments appeared in the first edition of this book we thought we might be deluged with complaints that we were being too flippant in our approach to the island's large scale art.

The reality is quite the reverse; we've been praised for making people think about the sculptures as unique pieces of art along with introducing 'Thingy' to the local language and encouraging the production of new Thingys.

FIRST IMPRESSIONS

If you are used to Mediterranean island destinations, or you've visited the western Canary Islands, your first arrival on the island might come as a bit of a shock. As your plane approaches the airport, you'll have an impression of barren starkness, relieved only by clusters and scatterings of cloned, squat white buildings, clustered thickly here and there on the coastline. But, give yourself a few hours to adapt, and you should begin to appreciate the subtleties of what is a chunk of African desert, overlain with volcanic spewings. The lava fields themselves have a certain weird beauty, and once you get over the withdrawal symptoms caused by the lack of trees, you'll find that Lanzarote is an island offering more colour and contrast than you might have assumed. The volcanic cones come in a variety of hues, and many parts of the coastline are dramatic and photogenic. Lanzarote might not appear at first glance to offer much variety or challenge for walkers; this book will change your opinion.

WHEN TO GO

If you want to walk, avoid the hot, dusty summer months of July, August and September. Be aware that, although Lanzarote has very little precipitation, you can hit some wet days; while completing research from February to April, there were four or five wet days. There were also a couple of *calimas*, the unpleasant hot, dust-laden east wind which picks up half the African deserts and then dumps it on the island. The skies darken with the suspended dust, and if you're a contact lens wearer or an asthma sufferer, you'll feel miserable. We wouldn't recommend walking in a *calima*, which can last anything from a couple of days to a week.

WHERE TO STAY

Almost all the accommodation is in the tourist resorts of **Costa Teguise**, **Puerto del Carmen** and **Playa Blanca**. The first two of these have the advantage of being close to the airport, having a reasonable bus service, and plenty of the usual tourist things, such as beaches, bars and shops. **Playa Blanca** is the place for you if you want to be near the ferry port for Fuerteventura, but it's a long way from everywhere else, and has a limited bus service. Sporting types can stay on the north coast at **Club La Santa** although there is not much distraction apart from within the complex itself.

GETTING AROUND THE ISLAND

There's a basic bus timetable in the back of this book, but be aware that these can change. Check on arrival, either at the Biosphere Information Office which faces you as you emerge from the baggage hall at the airport, in the tourist offices or online at www.arrecifebus.es. Some routes operate only on certain days and some towns and villages have only three or four buses a day. If you intend to use buses to access and return from walks, check the times first, and be prepared to use taxis.

Easiest is to hire a car, easily available and at reasonable rates. When using a car for linear walking routes, try to link up with like-minded walkers with another hire car and use the 2CSK method - see page 17. If you need a taxi when you are not near a tourist resort, ask in a bar and they will usually phone for you - but do buy a drink as well.

CÉSAR MANRIQUE

Within hours of the visitor's first arrival on Lanzarote, the influence of César Manrique (1919 - 1992) will already be obvious. The plain white, low-level buildings in traditional, unadorned style with their dark green doors and windows, and the sometimes startling sculptures that form traffic roundabouts, all bear witness to the singular effect this individual had - and still has - on the development of the island. Under his guidance, the **Jameos del Agua** caves were turned into a tourist attraction and an underground theatre. He was also the force behind the **Jardín de Cactus**, which although it contains the real thing, is oddly marked by an outrageously fake giant cactus in its car park. He had more than a hand in many other projects on the island, including the **Mirador del Río**, and the **Restaurante del Diablo** inside the **Montañas del Fuego** where volcanic energy is used to cook the food.

His main residence was **Taro de Tahiche**, north of **Arrecife**, now the **Fundación de César Manrique**, since his surreal death in a road traffic accident in 1992 on the very roundabout that he had alerted the authorities to as dangerous. His vision continues under the auspices of the El Guincho environmental group. In 1993, UNESCO recognised his efforts in preserving the natural environment of the island by declaring the entire island a World Biosphere Reserve.

PARQUE NACIONAL DE TIMANFAYA

An incredible eruption of cataclysmic proportions and lasting six years began on 1 September 1730. Centred in the south of the island, the **Montañas del Fuego** or Mountains of Fire, caused devastation to an area of 200 sq. km. The ground is still hot to the touch in places, and a party trick by the guides is to toss a dry bush into a crevasse whereupon it is instantly consumed by fire. The feeling is that the boiling molten magma is still close enough for discomfort. The **Restaurante del Diablo** built on the **Islote de Hilario** area within the park, uses the power of the volcano to barbecue the food, though it tastes no different to other forms of cooking and you do pay extra for this novelty.

Access to the park is restricted to cars and tour coaches (entrance fee payable), although there are guided walks available. If you would like to join one of these, apply at the **Centro de Visitantes** (Visitors' Centre) on the LZ 67 road, south of **Mancha Blanca**, in person or by phone on 928 840839. See Walk 18, 'Tremesana Guided Walk' for details. There's a tougher 'Ruta del Litoral' lasting about five hours and covering a distance of 9 kilometres which is arranged according to demand.

You can also take a coach tour from the parking area, taking in the weird volcanic landscapes, though you might find the multi-lingual commentary and taped music which accompany the tour irritating, and it is frustrating not to be have the freedom to walk independently in these unique surroundings.

LANZAROTE'S SALT

Lanzarote produces about one third of the salt it needs, but the industry is not as important as it once was. The **Salinas del Río**, (see Walk 37 'Salinas del Río') almost on the island's most north-westerly point, are thought to have been constructed in the 15th century and are shown on maps drawn in 1590. The quantities produced here were more than sufficient to serve the island's needs; the excess was sold to La Palma and Tenerife.

Until 1775, these salt pans were the only ones on Lanzarote, but from that time on several were constructed to cash in on the growing market. **Salinas del Agujero** were constructed in 1940, near **Los Cocoteros** which, together with **Salinas del Janubio** are the principal remaining commercial salt pans The most scenic are **Salinas del Janubio** which exists thanks to the volcanic eruptions of 1730, when molten lava formed the walls of the natural lake of **Laguna de Janubio**. Salt production has declined in the last few decades; now the *salinas* are important havens for bird life.

Salinas del Janubio

Cactus farm near Guatiza

CACTI & COCHINEAL
Naturalised in all the Canary Islands, Prickly Pear cactii (opuntia) were introduced as a hedging plant whose edible fruits are collected by those prepared to risk being impaled on its sturdy spikes; you may see Canarians collecting these bright red or orange fruits with the aid of wooden tongs.

Prickly Pears also proved to be the most popular host plant for the cochineal beetle, which led to a thriving cottage industry in the valuable dark red dye harvested from these insects which are dried and ground. The development of artificial colourings almost killed the industry, but in recent years some manufacturers - especially of drinks, foodstuffs and cosmetics - have returned to this natural dye.

The cochineal beetles give away their presence by the protective white powder that they exude around themselves as they feed off the cactus sap. There are few naturalised cacti in the Canaries without a few of these telltale signs of infestation, and in a few villages including **Guatiza** and **Mala** they are still farmed despite the extremely labour-intensive nature of the industry, each tiny bug being collected by hand.

GOATS
Goats are survivors, living on a diet of tough, wizened and spiny plants at which any sheep would turn up its nose. Ideal livestock in this arid and unforgiving landscape, an estimated 15,000 or so live happily on what might appear to be barren desert. It would be easy to make the assumption that they are wild, but most have owners, as the presence of goatherds proves. Traditionally a source of meat, milk, cheese, wool, skins, tallow for candles and a host of herbal cures and remedies, the goat was historically an essential factor in the survival of Lanzarote's early settlers. These days there is a healthy market for goat's cheese and meat and a modest demand for crafts using goat's wool and skins. You would be unlucky not to see a herd of these multi-patterned creatures while walking on the island, and you'll probably envy them their sure-footedness and easy tackling of slippery slopes.

THINGS TO DO

If you want a change from walking (or the beach) there are several attractions to visit. The island's best natural wonders have been turned into profit making ventures, including the **Montañas del Fuego** inside the **Parque Nacional de Timanfaya**, the **Jardín de Cactus**, the **Mirador del Río**, the **Jameos del Agua**, a huge volcanic tube inside which is a lake, restaurant, bars and a theatre, and the **Cueva de los Verdes**, another part of the same massive volcanic tube which has been kept in a more natural state. There are several museums for anything from traditional and contemporary art, wine, agriculture, Lanzarote emigrants and local crafts. There are boat trips for sightseeing, diving or fishing, or you could hop on the ferry to Fuerteventura from **Playa Blanca**, or see the tiny island of **La Graciosa**, reached by ferry from **Orzola** in about 25 minutes. Camel treks and horse riding are available, and the relatively flat terrain and quiet roads are ideal for cycling, with bicycle hire offered by several companies. **Costa Teguise** and **Puerto del Carmen** have golf courses.

Los Hervideros

Free attractions include the **Salinas del Janubio**, the coastline at **Los Hervideros** (the boiling springs), north of the salt pans where the sea boils and spouts through lava fissures. The jagged lava has been tamed into a series of narrow paths among the lava and

Charco de los Clicos

caves;   if the sea is rough, expect to get a shower as the sea is forced up through natural blowholes. Also worth a visit is the half volcanic crater of **Charco de los Clicos** near **El Golfo**.

PLANT LIFE

Trees are scarce on Lanzarote, and where they do grow, it is thanks to careful planting and sustained watering. Some of the best plantings are in hotel gardens, where they provide a valuable mini-habitat for bird and insect life. Because the volcanic history of the island is still relatively recent, swathes of its surface are still littered with lava in one of its forms. These areas of *malpaís* show signs of the process of breaking down into smaller particles that will eventually become soil, as the colourful colonies of lichen prove. In other areas where volcanic ash rather than rock and lava streams covered them, (such as **La Geria**, Walks 25&26), fertile soil lies beneath black duvets of fine ash, which serve to protect the roots of Malvasia grape vines, figs and other crops while drawing moisture from the cooler night air, which then percolates downwards. This method of mulching with a thick layer of ash has been adopted for agriculture of all kinds often used with the horseshoe-shaped low walls or *zocos* which give additional protection from the prevailing winds.

The dampest part of Lanzarote, the north, has the deepest and most workable soil. The little town of **Haría** (Walk 28, The Forgotten Trail, Walk 29 Barranco del Malpaso and Walk 30, Circuit of Haría), sits in a fertile bowl where many types of fruit and vegetable crops are grown. The whole valley is dotted with Phoenix canariensis palms, and the roadsides are sparsely lined by white or pale pink Tamarix africana.

The Haría Valley

Look in the north of the island, especially around the **El Risco de Famara** and **Haría** areas, for the island's own endemic miniature version of sea-lavender, Limonium puberulum. Easier to spot is the white tajinaste, Echium decaisnei which can reach 1½ metres in height, and the bright yellow dandelion-like Sonchus pinnatifidus. Another yellow giant is the fennel, Ferula lancerottensis, also an endemic. Mesembryanthemum crystallinum is a big name for the small, ground-hugging ice-plant which is common in many parts of the island, once used in the production of a type of soda.

2CSK - THE LINEAR SOLUTION

We've worked hard to ensure that our routes are as accessible as possible, though Lanzarote's landscape means that on our long linear routes we inevitably find ourselves a long way from our starting point. Walks 11, 14, 18, 21 (unofficial version), 24, 31 and 32 are just such routes. **2CSK** is our recommended solution to the problem of accessibility on linear routes. You need two walking couples/groups, each with its own hire car (2C).
• Get together and agree which linear routes you'll walk and when.
• On the day of the walk each group drives to one end of the linear route, locks the car, and starts walking the route.
• When the two groups meet, swap/exchange car keys (SK), and at the end of the walk drive the waiting hire car back to your agreed meeting point.

In practice, though, never underestimate the ability of the other group to become confused as to what they should be doing. You will only know if things have gone 'belly up' when you arrive at the end of that long route, having crossed with nobody, to find no car! However, when it works, it's a great way of seeing otherwise inaccessible regions of the island. The key to success is planning. Write everything down. Make sure both groups have a good map (Lanzarote Tour & Trail Map) and guide book. If you have mobiles, make sure each has the other's number. Write down the details of the other hire car and ask precisely where it has been parked when you meet.

USING GPS ON LANZAROTE

As the pioneers of using GPS for walking navigation, we should be singing the praises of the pin-point navigational accuracy that you get by using a GPS. However, all the routes in Walk! Lanzarote are so accurately described that following our routes is simply a matter of following the walk description. Even the two new routes which involve navigating across open, pathless landscape are straightforward; Walk 13, where after leaving **Las Breñas,** we simply head northeast across the gently sloping plain towards the LZ-701 road visible in the distance, while on Walk 33; when we leave the dirt track we simply head uphill until we see the tall red and white mast, then head for that.

A GPS may not be necessary, but is useful if you want to know exactly where you are on a walking route, and also for finding the start of a route, especially if it's your first visit to the island. With the walking route's waypoints loaded in your GPS, simply activate the 'Go To' function for Waypoint 1. Mapping GPS units and 3G/4G phones running GPS apps give you a real time moving map display. If you have the digital version of our Tour & Trail Map on your mapping GPS or phone, then you'll be able to see exactly where you are on all of our walking routes (except our Walk 27 town route in **Teguise**).

All the waypoints for Walk! Lanzarote walking routes are available as a free downloadable zip file. Locate the download page on our website, then download the zip file to your hard drive, unzip the file and you will have all the individual waypoint files in gpx file format; then simply load the files you want into your GPS or phone app.

If you are thinking of a GPS for walking navigation then our book **GPS The Easy Way** is available as a £4.99 book or as a free download in pdf format from our website.

Digital editions of our Tour & Trail Maps are available from Quo for the Lowrance Endura mapping GPS units, and Memory Map for their Adventurer series of mapping GPS units. If you already have a 3G phone then we suggest you consider GPS apps by MyTrails, Memory Map and Viewranger, all of whom supply our T&T Maps for their apps enabling you to use your phone offline as a full mapping GPS unit without incurring phone call or roaming charges. For more information see their websites.

SYMBOLS RATING GUIDE

 our rating for effort/exertion:-
1 very easy **2** easy **3** average
4 energetic **5** strenuous

 approximate **time** to complete a walk (compare your times against ours early in a walk) - does not include stopping time

 8km approximate walking **distance** in miles/kilometres

 250m / 850m approximate **ascents/descents** in metres (N=negligible)

 circular route

 linear route

 figure of eight route

 risk of **vertigo**

 refreshments (may be at start or end of a route only)

Walk descriptions include:
- timing in minutes, shown as (40M)
- compass directions, shown as (NW)
- heights in metres, shown as (1355m)
- GPS waypoints, shown as (Wp.3)

Notes on the text
Place names are shown in **bold text**, except where we refer to a written sign, when they are enclosed in single quotation marks. Local or unusual words are shown in *italics*, and are explained in the accompanying text.

The map sections used in this book are taken from **Lanzarote Tour & Trail Map** and aligned so that north is at the top of the page. Waypoint positions and numbers refer to the walking route shown in that map section.

Lanzarote Tour & Trail Map is a large scale (1:40,000 scale) full colour map. For more information on DWG publications, visit:

www.walking.demon.co.uk   www.dwgwalking.co.uk

Altitude

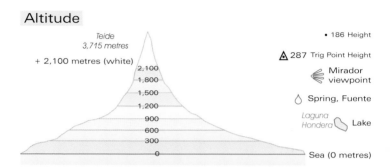

Roads, Tracks & Trails

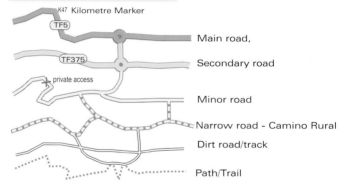

Walking Routes

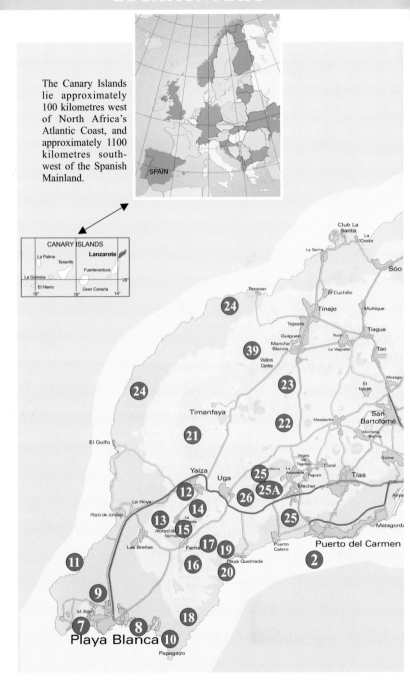

The Canary Islands lie approximately 100 kilometres west of North Africa's Atlantic Coast, and approximately 1100 kilometres south-west of the Spanish Mainland.

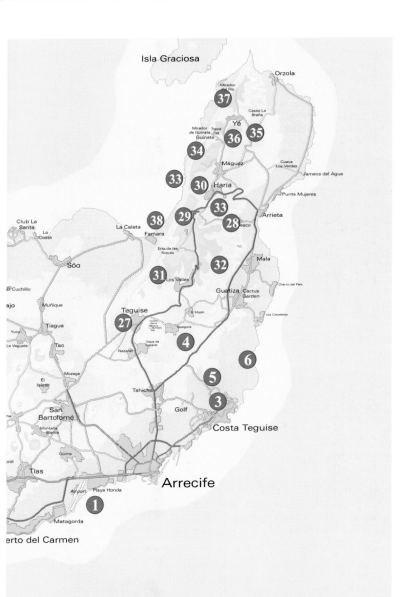

Remorseless sunshine combines with very low (zero) humidity, and a barren rock/lava/grit landscape covers much of the island. Protection against sunburn, sunstroke and dehydration should not be relaxed for even the easiest of routes.

BACKPACK

A 25-30 litre day pack or cyclist's pack should easily cope with all the equipment you think you will need for a day's walking. We suggest a pack with plenty of outside pockets. well-padded straps spread the load and a waist strap will stop the pack moving about. A ventilated back panel and/or stand-off frame helps clear sweat. Spend time adjusting the straps for a good fit.

FOOTWEAR

Underfoot conditions range from comfortable dirt tracks to walking trails, and some 'open ground' walking, on rock/lava, usually uneven. Whether you choose boots, shoes or sandals they must be up to the task. You need a hard sole with plenty of grip and a well padded foot-bed. Whichever footwear you choose, do make sure that you've broken them in.

SUN PROTECTION

Wear loose clothing and a comfortable sun hat that gives plenty of shade and stays on in windy conditions; 'Legionnaire' caps which protect neck and ears too. Use high-factor sun cream on all exposed skin and carry some in your pack for topping-up en-route. Wrap-round sunglasses protect eyes from UV radiation and from grit. When you take a break, sit in the shade.

WATER & FOOD

Dehydration is a real risk. When the sand-laden *calima* wind blows in from the Sahara, humidity drops to zero and the wind leeches moisture from you. Have a long drink before beginning the walk. Carry at least a couple of ½-litre water bottles add extra for longer, more strenuous routes. Even on short routes, carry survival rations; chocolate bars, dried fruit and the like provide welcome comfort when out in the wild.

MEDICAL KIT

Take antiseptic wipes, antiseptic cream, plasters, bandage and lip salve. Include tweezers, and a whistle to attract attention if you get into difficulties.

NAVIGATION

Don't compromise - buy and carry the best guide book and the best map. A compass is useful to orientate yourself at the start of a route and for general directions, but a GPS is far more useful - see Using GPS on Lanzarote.

CLOTHING

Choose loose comfortable clothing and add a lightweight, rainproof jacket to your back pack. The island might be mostly desert, but it does rain sometimes.

OTHER EQUIPMENT

Digital cameras generally weigh far less than their film equivalents and a 3G phone is even lighter. A monocular is half the weight of a pair of binoculars. Money (refreshments, taxis, public telephones, drinks machines etc.) is also recommended.

Bear in mind that the times given in each route description are the actual walking times that we recorded while walking the routes ourselves - you might cover the ground more quickly or slowly. Check your progress against ours early in the walk, and you will soon be able to estimate the time you'll need relative to ours. Also remember that the times given are for continuous walking, so you'll need to add more time for rest stops, picnics, admiring the views, taking photos etc.

If you are new to walking, or out of condition, then we suggest that you choose one of the coastal promenade walks; (Walks 1&2, **Puerto del Carmen** to **Arrecife**, Walk 3 **Costa Teguise** Walks 7&8, **Playa Blanca**). A couple of other routes will also break you in gently; Walk 22 to **Montaña Cuervo**, or Walk 27 around the old town of **Teguise**. In some cases, there's the choice of a short version of longer or more challenging routes.

To experience the strange volcanic desert landscapes, try Walk 11 on the **Rubicón** plain, or Walk 24 which combines lava fields with the coastline of **Timanfaya**. There are some beautiful beach routes, for example to **Papagayo** on Walk 10. If mountains are more your style, there's the easy **Montaña Roja** one hour route (Walk 9), or routes out of **Femés** taking in the peaks in this beautiful region; one 'mountain route not to miss' is Walk 39 **Caldera Blanca**. And if you thought Lanzarote was lacking in lush vegetation, we're confident that the routes in the north of the island, for example Walk 28 'The Forgotten Trail', our new Walk 29 **Barranco del Malpaso** or Walk 34 **Helechos Circular**, will change your opinion.

Read through your chosen route a couple of times before setting out and make sure you have appropriate clothing, equipment and refreshments with you.

SAFETY

- Don't attempt high altitude routes in severe weather. Be prepared to abandon a route and turn back if bad weather closes in.
- Don't walk alone - or at least let someone know where you are planning to walk.
- Wear appropriate clothing and footwear, and carry the right equipment
- Take frequent drinks of water.
- Shade is scarce on Lanzarote. Protect yourself from the sun.
- Start out early enough - allow plenty of time to complete the route before dark.
- Stay on the route. If it is impassable, retrace your steps.

Since opening back in 2004 the coastal promenade linking **Matagorda** to **Arrecife** has been improved: the original boardwalk has been replaced by a broad tarmac path for walkers and cyclists along with the addition of seating and even a new 'thingy'. These improvements have helped make this Lanzarote's most popular easy walking and strolling route requiring no more than suitable footwear, clothing and sun protection. Beach side bars **at Playa Honda** mean you can conveniently stop for refreshment at the half way stage of the route. If you find 9+ kilometres of walking more than enough, your arrival in **Arrecife** close by the bus terminus makes it easy to catch a **Puerto del Carmen** bus back for your return.

The new 'thingy'

2/3   2 H   9½ km   N N   2

Acces s by bus: Take the N°2 **Puerto del Carmen** bus from **Arrecife** and alight at the first stop in **Matagorda**, then walk down past the **Sol Lanzarote Hotel**. From **Puerto del Carmen**, alight at the first stop after the roundabout at the end of the beach road and follow the coastal pavement (E and add 0.7 kilometres) or at the stop by **Sol Lanzarote** (see appendices at the back of this book for timetables).

Access by car:
When you see the **Sol Lanzarote Hotel**, take the road running down the western side of the hotel, **Calle Agonal** where we've always found plenty of on-street parking, even at weekends.

On foot from Puerto del Carmen:
Simply walk down to the sea front and follow the beach-side pavement eastwards to meet our official start. You can walk from the 'old town' on promenade and the beach road pavement, adding 5.5 kilometres and 1 hour to distance and time above.

From the end of **Calle Agonal** (Wp1 0M) we follow the broad beachside promenade east; this section was once a road, pedestrianised for over a decade now. An easy stroll - the whole route is easy strolling - brings us to a rotating 'thingy' (Wp.2 6M) installed since our first edition of this route. Our next feature is a lava tower (lifeguard and red cross station) shortly before coming to the start of the upgraded section of walkway (Wp.3 12M) beside a grey rock 'thingy' set in a roundabout at the end of the road. Now we're striding out to leave tourism behind, past stone seats set in the lava wall to pass an aerial-bedecked building before coming to the end of the runway (Wp.4 19M), a popular spot with plane watchers, the big jets making an impressive sight when taking off over us.

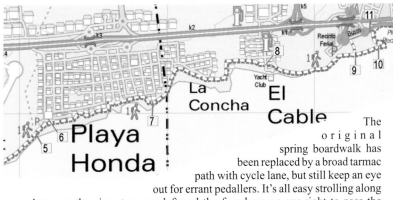

The original spring boardwalk has been replaced by a broad tarmac path with cycle lane, but still keep an eye out for errant pedallers. It's all easy strolling along between the airport on our left and the foreshore on our right to pass the 'cozzie optional' small beach of **Playa de Guasimeta** followed by *zoco* style sunbathing shelters as we start closing with the **Playa Honda** urbanisation. Our path brings us along to cross a wooden bridge over a gully (Wp.5) to come onto the pebbledash slabs of **Playa Honda**'s promenade and the welcome sight of **Bar Mercedes** (Wp.6 44M) facing the impressive sweep of golden sand; if you do miss this refreshment opportunity, there is another at **Bar Mesana** in a few metres.

The second stage of our excursion is along the sea front of **Playa Honda**, again once a road but now more popular as a promenade - except for those owners whose garages face the beach. Our broad walkway twists along the edge of the beach, passing a pair of houses on the seaward side pre-dating the current planning laws, and a clutch of bars (Wp.7) before swinging left to round a crescent of sand. Here you can short cut across the sand, though our choice is the easy promenade stroll around the lagoon inside the sand bar, passing another beach entry before a short climb is followed by steps down to continue on a crude concrete surface - funny how the worst section of the promenade fronts the flashiest houses.

Housing ends as the concrete swings inland as we come onto a recently finished section; being much easier than our original short cut across the beach past a true beach-house before coming back onto the official walkway. Back to easy strolling, we leave the sea for a while to pass inland of **El Cable Yacht Club** (Wp.8). Keeping straight ahead, we go right onto pebbledash slabs and then left to come onto the wide brick paved promenade for our final section into **Arrecife**.

.. a seating area that could pass for a thingy ..

The broad brick promenade is built directly on the sea front rocks, waves crashing against the wall and spraying our route as we close rapidly on the previously distant **Arrecife** as we pass a seating area that could pass for a 'thingy'. Passing an extensive car park and **Biosfera** centre on our left, the neo-classical *Cabildo* building comes into sight on our left along with a large rusty 'thingy' as we pass the Intercambiador bus station. An easy stroll brings us up to the start of the thematic park though unfortunately the 'ships vents' waste bins are still un-emptied making for a shabby entrance to the island's capital. At a 'muse' (Wp.9) - almost a 'thingy' - you could short-cut left across the park, though our full route goes on past the 'shipwreck' to the prow (Wp.10 95M) of the 'boat' theme park before swinging left around **Playa Reducto** to meet the road (Wp.11 100M), just to the east of the Intercambiador bus station.

The muse at Wp.9

Arrecife had a rather scruffy air when we were researching the original edition but has been undergoing some renovations in the interim. The shops still close for the 13.00 to 16.00 siesta; even so, strolling round the pedestrianised shopping streets where modern shops jostle with traditional establishments is an entertaining experience at any hour. Following the seafront road, on the pavement, we pass the refurbished **Gran Arrecife Hotel** (previously a notable eyesore) and yacht club before coming to the Tourist Information Office whose helpful staff can give a proper insight into the town's delights.

Lanzarote's southern coast provides a popular walking route from **Puerto del Carmen** to the new resort and marina of **Puerto Calero**, an easy stroll, after which we continue on to reach **Playa Quemada**, a rather scruffy coastal village though graced by *tipico* bar/restaurants. Easy rather than spectacular, this route provides a good introduction to the island's countryside and is ideal as a stroll out, taking a drink in the new marina before continuing on to **Playa Quemada** for a relaxed lunch. Repeat the procedure on the way back for a laid back day's walking.

Originally a cross-country ramble on narrow dirt trails, this is now a truly manicured route graced with wide pavements/path and frequent stone seating as far as **Puerto Calero**. New crossings of **Barranco de Quiquere** and into **Puerto Calero** avoid the 'inland diversions' of our original route so making this a good strolling route for everyone with comfortable footwear.

Access by bus:
N°2 **Arrecife** to **Puerto del Carmen**, N°3 **Costa Teguise** to **Puerto del Carmen**, N°6 **Playa Blanca** to **Puerto del Carmen**. Return by bus N°25 from **Puerto Calero** (stops at **Puerto del Carmen**, **Arrecife** & **Costa Teguise**, see appendices at the back of this book for timetables).

We start out from the old port at the western end of **Puerto del Carmen** (Wp.1 0M) taking the steps up by the **El Veradero Restaurant** to **Calle Los Infantes** which we follow to its end by the **Rincón Apartments**.

> **Short Walk**
> To **Puerto Calero** marina and return (2 hours, 9 kilometres).

Climbing the zigzag stair

From the end of the cul-de-sac we climb the rope-handrailed stair to come to the start of the coastal walkway (Wp.2). It used to be an unpromising start, climbing up a steep rock bluff, but now the 'rope/slope'zigzag ascent brings us onto a broad pavement which runs along below villas.

Passing a couple of 'gazebo' style seating areas, it's an easy stroll above the sea to the end of the paving (Wp.3), continuing on a broad dirt path heading out into the countryside. Navigation couldn't be simpler as we follow the broad path lined with low posts that runs along the top of the cliffs, before swinging inland to cross a rocky inlet (Wp.4)

Our route runs out of the inlet into a flat barren landscape dotted with squat-walled villas as the path comes back to the cliffs for us to pass an abandoned cliff-side villa (N°17) before coming to the lava-walled gardens of villas at the entrance to **Barranco de Quiquere** (Wp.5 30M), a veritable oasis when set against this barren landscape. Low lava walls protect us from the cliffs as we swing into the *barranco* to discover another major improvement to this route.

.. the broad path lined with low posts ..

Crossing the *barranco*

Originally, crossing the *barranco* involved an inland diversion or a tricky scramble down to the its floor, then another tricky climb out and around the seaward side of the villas.

Now we have a gentle stepped descent before crossing the watershed followed by a steady climb up the manicured broad path; there's even a seat half way up if you want to take a break, plus a collection of stone seats just as we reach the crest beyond the last villa - now, how thoughtful is that?

If this is your first southern walk, allow yourself the luxury of taking in the distant views. Inland, the central massif finishes at the pass to **La Geria**, while the large building set on the final ridge is a *parapente* launch point. Depending on the winds, you might see whole flocks of these colourful fragile fliers gliding down to their landing strip inland from **Puerto Calero**.

To the right of the pass is the 'pencil-point' peak of **Montaña de Guardilama** which offers Lanzarote's most spectacular viewpoint to those fit

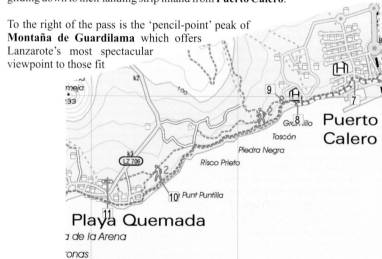

enough to brave the ascent; our **La Geria** route (Walk 25) offers the opportunity to experience those lofty delights. Ahead are the misty southern mountains which rise almost sheer from the **Rubicón** plain. The antennaed peak of **Atalaya de Femés** sits above the pretty village of **Femés**, our centre for some adventurous walking routes amongst the peaks and *barrancos* of this little-known region. Yes, there's plenty of exciting walking ahead of you.

On the Paseo Maritimo

Our broad path takes us along low cliffs set above a lava plateau foreshore before dropping into a small *barranco* and then climbing back onto the cliffs. Originally there was a myriad of quad bikers' tracks and trails across this area but the new official path offers easier strolling. We come up to overlook **Puerto Calero** marina at a path junction (Wp.6 54M); previously we had to detour inland and round the streets before meeting the marina's **Paseo Maritimo** promenade. Now we take advantage of the new stone path descending into the *barranco* to cross the marina access road onto the **Paseo Maritimo**; the *paseo* climbs up to overlook the marina as we stroll along to its main entrance. (Wp.7 61M).

Continuing on towards Playa Quemada

Puerto Calero offers a selection of shops, cafes, bars and restaurants set against a backdrop of expensive nautical hardware; just the place for a leisurely break, whether you plan to continue on to **Playa Quemada** or simply to return to **Puerto del Carmen**. There's also the option of returning by bus from **Puerto Calero** on bus N°25 (via **Puerto del Carmen** and **Arrecife** to **Costa Teguise**).

The rock stairway before Wp.9

For our continuation on to **Playa Quemada**, we take the **Paseo Maritimo** (0M) from beside the marina entrance. We follow this wide elegant walkway as it undulates along out past the marina, a number of flights of stairs giving access down to the foreshore before the walkway turns inland up to a T-junction (Wp.8 10M) at the **Hotel Hespería**.

Although it looks like a dead end, we go left (W) to walk past the restaurant entrance onto a small rock headland with marine rope railing.

We follow the rope down steps to cross a tiny artificial beach and climb a rock stairway that brings us up to the western end of the hotel from where we come inland beside the hotel to pick up a track (Wp.9) that curves up over the next headland.

The dusty track takes us into an undulating landscape, quite adventurous compared to the manicured walkway to **Puerto Calero**. Staying on the track, we head towards the coast. This is another area used by quad bikers, resulting in a myriad of tracks and trails. To avoid confusion, keep to the coastal track/trail as we go through a series of gentle ascents and descents to head westwards across small hills and shallow valleys; when a track turns inland a walking trail links us to the next track section. Only when we walk up a longer than usual slope do we come into view of the first houses of **Playa Quemada**; this point (Wp.10) is grandly shown as a trig point of 22 metres on military maps, but is hardly noticeable on the ground.

Following the track, we come to the first houses, the track becoming tarmac for an easy stroll down the first street to a small square. Then it's downhill past the beach front houses to a restaurant (Wp.11 32M) where you could walk down the beach front instead of the road. Cutting through to the beach, we stroll along to the end of the houses to come onto the tarmac as it heads inland to the **7 Islas** and **La Casita** bar/restaurants.

As we sit on one of these terraces and take refreshment, we can absorb the charm of this informal settlement of small houses and weekender homes. Some might describe its rather disorganised style as scruffy, but there's no doubting its quaintness. Just as the track to **Puerto Calero** contrasts with the path to **Playa Quemada**, so does this settlement's casual approach contrast with the 'organised' development of the marina; in one short walk we've experienced three contrasting coastal settlements; just pick the one that seems most agreeable to yourself.

Take your time relaxing before returning to the resort by your outward route.

Our coastal promenade walks are popular, ideal when you don't want a day out in the wild landscapes or with families as a group stroll, but they receive very little or nil official recognition.

So imagine our surprise on arriving in **Costa Teguise** to find our promenade route had been officially adopted and then extended by the making of trails, into a 10km route with two shorter options. Talking to people walking the long (red) route, they seemed pleased by this official new resource as evidenced by one conversation. "We walked it one way round yesterday. Now we're doing it this way round."

The overall route might be a bit contrived in places where trails have been constructed alongside pavements, but as a way to see the overall resort, both its seafront and its back side, it cannot be beaten. Another consequence of the official route is that previously abandoned areas of the resort have been cleaned up with some new gardens planted. If we have one criticism - it makes us feel quite mean to even have one - it is that once we leave the seafront, refreshment opportunities are non-existent so take water with you.

If you wonder why we need to detail an official route, it's because a number of the signboards and wayposts had already been vandalised when we arrived. No one can destroy or vandalise a walk description or the waypoints that accompany it. This route (well, three routes) deserves preservation for encouraging holidaymakers into the edge of the 'wild'.

An official mapboard

It's unusual for us to not include timings along a route; however, as this is a strolling town walk with various options, they would serve no useful purpose in this case.

* on seafront only. However Helga's Kitchen, specialising in coffee and cakes, located behind the tourist information office, is recommended though not on the direct walking route.

Access from within Costa Teguise:
Simply walk from your accommodation to your nearest point on the walking route and start your adventure there.

Access by bus:
Route Nº01 runs between **Arrecife** and **Costa Teguise** (stops at **Las Caletas** in western **Costa Teguise** and **Hotel Salinas**, in the resort's east, plus 5 other

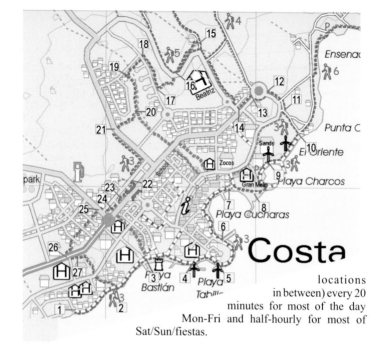

locations in between) every 20 minutes for most of the day Mon-Fri and half-hourly for most of Sat/Sun/fiestas.

Access by car:

There is on-street car parking on the street accessing the western end of the promenade, plus extensive car parking in the inland side of the commercial centres facing **Playa Cucharas**.

Starting at the turning circle at the end of **Calle de los Volcanes** (Wp.1) we take the broad paved promenade heading east to pass some newly installed yellow exercise machines shortly before coming to the new path junction with the official red route (Wp.2), our return route on the full circular. Villas give way to the stark face of the **Hotel Las Coronas** before we pass on to the much more inviting **Playa Bastián** where the green route trail joins the promenade (Wp.3) followed by walkways accessing the resort and a 'martello' tower which acts as a lifeguard/red cross station for the beach.

At a pedestrian roundabout we keep right to follow the promenade past the **Hotel Punta Jabillo** and a replica windmill overlooking **Playa Tabillo** (Wp.4). Round the beach, we pass the **Neptuno Commercial Centre** before coming to another replica windmill (Wp.5) opposite the **Apartamentos Nautilus**. The brick paved promenade changes to eroded pebbledash as we round the point to come in sight of the tall 'thingys' which dominate **Playa Cucharas**, the resort's main beach. As we cross the port's access road (Wp.6) at a roundabout you might want to take the short stroll along the dock to examine the thingys from close quarters.

Playa Cucharas is a family-friendly beach with calm water, thanks to the dock and breakwater. Opposite the beach across the promenade is another matter with a mixture of Brit bars and cheap-looking shops selling tourist tat; even the imaginatively named 'Sunburnt Arms' pub is long gone. Past a rusting thingy and Brit and Irish bars, we come to the head of the beach where we have the option to take the walkways up to the parking area, then go left along the parking to find **Helga's Kitchen** tucked away in a small courtyard behind the tourist office, returning to the main route after indulging in coffee and cake. A collection of oversize plumbing parts on the seaward side of the promenade could possibly rank as a thingy as we traverse the main beach area to a junction (Wp.7) where a path leads left to the commercial centre while we continue right for the final section of the beach out to the breakwater (Wp.8).

Our route curves left to the breakwater protecting **Playa Los Charcos** where going left we follow the promenade around the beach, a much classier area including a replica windmill (Wp.9) and an inland lagoon which is part of **Sands Beach Villas**, then we're heading out into the country past an original windmill, dating from the sea salt era, to the end of the promenade (Wp.10) where we turn left following the 'red' route.

The trail at the resort's eastern edge

Heading inland on a dirt track, we come to the first of the contrived trails (Wp.11) at the side of **Avenida de las Islas** which we follow to cross the **Ancones** dirt road before coming onto the pavement alongside a large roundabout (Wp.12).

Here the 'red' route goes SW on pavement marked by two waypoints before returning to a contrived trail at the third waypost (Wp.13) which parallels the pavement of **Avenida de las Palmeras** (SW) until we turn right at the next junction (Wp.14). We head along **Atalaya** (NNW) towards **Hotel Beatrix** where, after a hundred metres, we have the choice of continuing on pavement or the dirt trail which parallels it. Pavement or trail, we head (NW) towards the expanding edifice of the hotel, looking more giant aquarium than upmarket hotel as we get closer, to where the road swings left for us to continue to a trail junction (Wp.15); here our Walk 5 comes down the trail to join us. Going left on the newly-made red route, we climb up a small escarpment to the graffitied ruin of a cottage, along with the remains of wayposts and notice board. The red trail then drops down to below road level in a picky descent before climbing beside the pavement to meet the road at the top of its gradient (Wp.16).

The 'green' river

The section between waypoints 15 & 16 is very contrived and you could skip the inconvenience of it by simply walking up the pavement, as we do for Walk 5, to the trail's continuation. A barren dry gully is piped under the road where we cross, the gully a surprising bright green 'river' of plant life, completely stuffed with Euphorbias on its far side of the road; in these barren surroundings this slash of green plant life is unusual.

Taking the red trail, we pass a faint path off to our left before arriving at a waypost alongside **Calle Garajonay (**Wp.17) which our trail follows (N) until it crosses the street (Wp.18). Now we come down to cross a large dry watercourse, then gently ascend to the second feature of the official route, an old water cistern (Wp.19); that ruined graffitied cottage was the first feature. It's not much of a water cistern; you'll see a far more impressive one on Walk 36, but as it was there , we've included it. Leaving the cistern behind, we stroll down alongside the dry watercourse to a trail junction (Wp.20) where the blue and green official routes meet the red route.

Here you can shortcut back into the resort by following the blue and green route in reverse as it continues (SE) alongside the dry watercourse to cross **Calle La Laguna** and then on to a signboard on **Avenida de las Palmeras**. Here the official route goes left to a zebra crossing then continues as a trail heading alongside tourist developments (SE) to come onto **Avenida de las Islas Canarias** opposite the extensive car parking for **Centro Comercial Las Cucharas**. If you are heading for **Helga's Kitchen** then turn right and then left, just before the tourist office.

From the junction (Wp.20), we take the combined route (SW) as our trail scales a small ridge before running down to cross **Ruta del Norte** (Wp.21) on a zebra crossing with signboards on each side of the road. Once again our manicured trail parallels the street, even turning right at the road junction to parallel **Calle Crotos**, before going right for a couple of metres for us to come onto the pavement just before **Residencial Las Gaviotas**. To find our trail's continuation we walk down the pavement (SW) to cross the street on a zebra crossing where we find the trail again (Wp.22).

Our trail drops down to cross the street just north of the road bridge and then climbs again to street level before coming to an unmarked junction (Wp. 23) where we need to go left to cross a street before our route leads onto the pavement of **Avenida de las Palmeras** for us to walk along to a junction of the official routes (Wp.24).

Aloe vera between the villas

From the official junction, the green (shortest) route heads left (SE) across the **Avenida**, crossings **Avenida del Mar** before arriving on the seafront promenade at Wp.3 offering us a shortcut finish option.

Red/blue route goes right on a trail that crosses **Avenida del Golf** (Wp.25) for us to walk through tightly-packed villa developments on a concrete path. Keeping straight ahead (SE) and ignoring paths off into the villas we cross three small streets, plus a children's play area with seats, before emerging into the open on the trail's continuation for us to come down to **Avenida Las Palmeras** again, which we cross on the zebra (Wp.26).

Newly-planted gardens after Wp.27

Across the main road, we walk along the pavement towards the resort (E) to a waypost indicating our trail's continuation (Wp.27). What used to be a scruffy piece of waste ground has been transformed by new gardens and seating which we pass on our way to crossing the **Avenida del Mar** on a zebra crossing.

Onto the final section of our route, again the waste ground has been improved by landscaping and planting of endemic species, making for a picturesque stroll down to meet the seafront promenade (Wp.2). Now we simply turn right to retrace our outward route back to our start (Wp.1) at **Calle de los Volcanes**.

4 SUNDAY MARKET SPECIAL - CAMINO EL CHARCO

With the advent of the car, many of Lanzarote's commerce routes were upgraded from donkey trails to tarmac roads. When Lanzarote was first colonised, pirate raids dictated establishing the capital at **Teguise**, protected by the **Castillo de Santa Bárbara**. From here routes ran down to the coast; one passing through the small settlement of **Teseguite** and then straight down to **Salinas El Charco**. Refrigeration largely killed the sea salt market, but this old donkey trail route is still shown on some maps. This is one old route which still survives, though the new **Tahiche-Mala** road necessitates a short diversion through a tunnel.

Sunday is the day to walk this route using a 'market special' bus, seeing the island's busiest street market before setting out on the old 'salt trail'.

Access by bus

Sunday market specials go from **Costa Teguise** (Nº11), **Puerto del Carmen** (Nº12), and **Playa Blanca** (Nº13); see appendices in the back of this book for timetables).

> **Short Walk**
> To **Castillo de Santa Bárbara** and return, (ascents/descents 110 metres).

Our starting point is at the start of the access road to **Castillo de Santa Bárbara** (Wp.1 0M). If you are coming from the market, then make your way to the main road, cross over and walk up the pavement to reach our 'official' start. With the old castle above us we have a slogging ascent up the tarmac (SE) between storm-water eroded earth banks. As we ascend we are looking

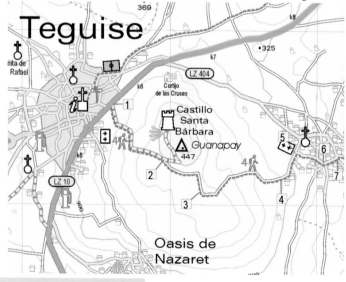

for a faint dirt track leaving the tarmac (Wp.2) which comes just before the road gets even steeper.

Gratefully, we leave the steepening tarmac to stroll along the narrow track between stone walls as it contours around the hill to come to cultivated fields contrasting with the generally barren landscape. Views open up over **Teseguite** and down to the coast as our track goes right to go around another area of storm-water eroded earth banks.

...views open up over Teseguite ...

Keeping to the main track (Wp.3), we swing left towards **Teseguite** to stroll gently downhill with extensive views expanding over the valley and up to the **Ermita de las Nieves** and radomes of Walk 31 'Capital Route - Haría to Teguise'. Our track swings downhill through the sunburnt landscape to bring us onto a tarmac street (Wp.4) and the first houses of **Teseguite**.

Teseguite might be a small settlement, but it can be confusing to navigate to find our exit route. Going left, we stroll down (NNE) to the second junction (Wp.5) marked by a 'palm tree' roundabout outside the cemetry, where we go right (E). We stroll gently downhill to cross over a village street, and pass **Casarino** on our right before coming to the next crossroads (Wp.6), where we go left (E).

It is downhill again to a T-junction (Wp.7) at the end of **Calle Revuelta**, where we go left and immediately right on **Calle Cadina** to come along to another T-

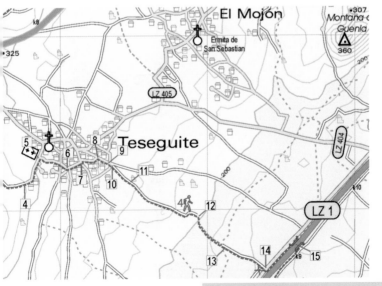

junction (Wp.8). Here we go right to start our exit into the country. At a junction (Wp.9) with 'Finca Luna' signed left, we go right, and where the tarmac lane swings right, we go straight ahead on a dirt track (Wp.10), the **Camino El Charco -** well, we did warn you it could be confusing.

We head out into the country between stone walls, passing a troglodyte style hut (Wp.11) to come into an area littered by a 'rain of stones'. It's downhill on the faint track, and after it swings left and right views open up across the sloping plain to **Montaña Corona** with **Costa Teguise** peeking round its base. Water erosion has washed away sections of the track as cultivated fields start on our left, just before the track runs out at a triangular field (Wp.12).

To find our onward route we go right across the edge of the field to go through a gap in a 'pile of stones' wall to find a faint trail heading down towards **Montaña Corona** along a gully. We pick our way down the shallow gully between fields to come out into the open; ahead a pair of cultivated fields stands out in the barren landscape. Keeping the water runoff on our right, we are back to easy strolling, our trail crossing the runoff

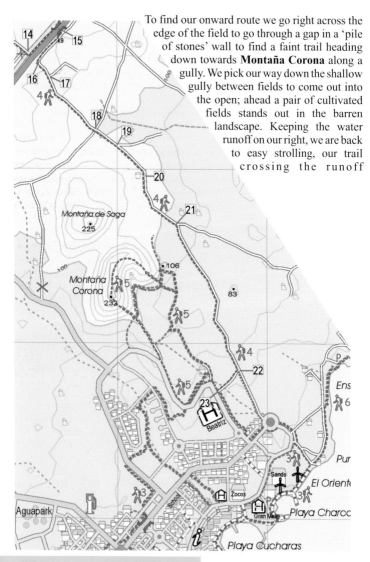

(Wp.13) and becoming better defined as we come to the cultivated fields. Now we simply keep straight ahead on the track, passing a pylon and then a 'bedstead' gated property on our right where the track becomes more used, to come down to meet the old main road (Wp.14).

Originally our route went straight across the old main road, but the new road is wider, faster and busier. To avoid any risk we go left (NE) on the old road to a tunnel under the new road (Wp.15) where we come onto remains of the old road. Going right, we continue alongside the new road on a track to come back to the line of the **Camino El Charco** (Wp.16). Obstacle passed, we are back to simple navigation as we follow a track heading towards **Montaña Corona** (SSE) and the coast, passing a minor track off to our left (Wp.17) and a pair of ruins before topping a rise where our track runs down to cultivated fields and a crossroads of tracks (Wp.18).

Coming down to the crossroads from the new road it is very noticeable how the land has changed. Above the main road the land is cheerfully barren, but below, it's as if this forgotten plain is cowering beneath the dominant heights of **Caldera** and **Tahiche**. Grey is the dominant colour, relieved a little by the spiny grey-green Lanzarote Fire Bush (Launaea arborescens) which dominates the long-abandoned fields in this harsh landscape.

At least it is easy walking, passing a minor track (Wp.19) as we come gently uphill past cultivated fields to the unexpected sight of a house. Passing the house (Wp.20) and then another track off left to a field, we walk alongside a stone wall to come over a small rise; views open up to the ocean, though **Costa Teguise** is hidden behind the bulk of **Montaña Corona**. We drop down to cross a water runoff (Wp.21) where a faint track goes straight ahead, while our track swings right.

Approaching Costa Teguise

It's a featureless *malpais* littered with stones, our track changing to a more comfortable sand base as we curve towards **Costa Teguise**. An easy stroll brings us back onto the *malpais* at a small rise which brings the sea and **Costa Teguise** into view.

Our track becomes fainter as we cross a small water runoff (Wp.22) and then come up to see our faint track running across towards the **Hotel Beatrix** reception. The track gets even rougher as we pick our way down to step gratefully onto the pavement (Wp.23) outside this large hotel.

Once in town, there's the option to pick up our Walk 3 Costa Teguise Circular for those who'd like more walking.

5 MONTAÑA CORONA

While **Playa Blanca** has its **Montaña Roja**, **Costa Teguise** has **Montaña Corona**. Although the peaks differ by only 30 metres altitude, their natures are quite different. **Corona** might only be 232 metres high, but it is quite a tricky peak with a steep, pathless, final ascent and a slippery, shale-covered path descent. These two sections are joined by a ridge top walk around the rim of the *caldera* which might upset vertigo sufferers, and certainly should not be attempted in windy weather.

Those are the bad points, but for experienced walkers the views from the top fully justify the difficult ascent, and the ridge top walk is a pleasure for the confident. In windy weather, and for anyone unsure of tackling the ascent/ridge/descent, we have a low level short walk option suitable for all. Our Walk 3 Costa Teguise Circular links with this route.

Access by car: Park on the road past the massive **Hotel Beatriz** before the road swings left.

Access by bus: N°1 **Arrecife** to **Costa Teguise**, N°3 **Puerto del Carmen** via **Arrecife** to **Teguise**, N°61 **Puerto del Carmen** to **Playa Blanca**. From the most easterly bus stop (near **Hotel Salinas** on **Avenida Islas Canarias**, off **Avenida del Mar**) take pavements approximately NW to the **Hotel Beatriz**. See appendices at the back of this book for timetables.

> **Short Walk**
> Follow main route to the trail crossroads at Wp.4, then turn right to follow the lower trail as it contours around the *caldera* to the trail crossroads at Wp.8; then resume the main route.

Starting out on the western pavement (Wp.1 0M), we walk away from the resort, a ruin ahead of us on a small spur as the road and pavement swing left to climb past a pretty valley on our right, contrasting with the harsh *malpais* elsewhere. The spiny aulaga or Lanzarote firebush (Launaea arborescens) and saltbush (Suaeda vermiculata) invade the pavement as we climb up beside Walk 3's trail; then crossing Walk 3's route as the road swings right for us to walk through the largely barren *malpais* in a gentle ascent. Our pavement climbs up to a crest, and as it curves left we step off onto a jeep track (Wp.2 14M).

The track runs across open ground toward a gap in a stone wall. Passing a small trail off to our right (Wp.3), we climb up to the gap (20M) to find two large stone cairns which mark the trail to the base of **Montaña Corona**. It is easy walking along the trail to pass a large cairn and stone designs, better seen from the peak, to arrive at a crossroads

Montaña Corona stands out clearly ahead

of trails (Wp.4 24M).

For our Short Walk, turn right here and follow the trail round the *caldera* to the large stone cairn on a spur.

Montaña Corona looks both big and steep from this viewpoint, so girding our loins we set off up the lower slope on the stony trail, easier as an ascent than descent. The trail zigzags, more for artistic reasons than for any practical use, as we take frequent stops on this 'puff and grunt' climb. Our path disappears as we come onto bedrock, those stone designs by the crossroads much clearer from this elevated position. Our ascent is not vertiginous in the normal sense, but is developing into a steep almost scrambling climb; face the slope not the views when taking a break. We come slowly up past small volcanic blowholes, heading for the highest point above us, until finally we come up onto the summit of **Montaña Corona** (Wp.5 50M).

After that slightly unnerving climb, we gratefully take in the extensive views. Although we are only at 232 metres altitude, the low plains give the impression of a much higher altitude. Thoughtfully the rocks on the summit make for comfortable seating allowing us to enjoy a break before tackling the descent.

From the high point our return route is along the rock ridge of the *caldera*, a far more comfortable open ground route than our earlier ascent. We set off, picking our way carefully over the rocks and edge round a large boulder; this is definitely a 'Stop, and look at the view' section of the route.

... Montaña de Saga is a beautiful cone of reds and browns ...

Montaña de Saga is a beautiful cone of reds and browns to the north of us as we cross a broad rock cap to the ridge (Wp.6) before negotiating a trench through the ridge by caves. We are now curving south and descending through rough terrain to the second height point (Wp.7 62M).

A grit/shale path leads straight down the slope towards the large stone cairn on the saddle below, the path zigzagging as it loses height but this is still a very picky, slippery descent before arriving at a crossroads of trails (Wp.8 78M) just above the big stone cairn; our short walk option arriving here from the west.

Most walkers now plunge past the cairn and down the slippery, picky, loose shale trail to the flood plain fifty metres below, but if like us you have had enough of uncomfortable descents then we have a slightly longer but much more civilised alternative. From the crossroads we go left (N) on a narrow trail which curves round the mountain to a faint path junction (Wp.9 81M) where we keep right to descend amongst the foothills as our trail curves towards the resort. A faint trail goes onto a low rise as we continue down the small valley to cross its water runoff, where our trail is reduced to a trace crossing the flood plain towards a small cairn of stones (Wp.10 89M) where we meet the main path.

There are traces of paths almost everywhere on the flood plain, and the low ridges and big mountain offer no navigational sighting points; just the sort of country where GPS waypoint (or PNF) navigation scores highly. From the cairn we follow the sandy trail (SSW) to a junction where we go right and then a path joins us from the left, shortly followed by a path off to our right. We keep straight on the main path to close with old stone walls lining the valley, where we start climbing gently up past terraces abandoned millennia ago; do not pay any attention to white painted supposed cairns, as these are land boundary markers. Despite carrying Alan's route on a second GPS we disbelieve the faint path going up by a wall to climb up onto a low ridge (Wp.11 99M) where **Costa Teguise** comes into view.

Ahead a path runs across to the wall (Wp.3 on our outward route) while we go left on a fainter trail to meet a stone wall (Wp. 12) where we swing right (S) to head towards the **Hotel Beatriz**. Our trail heads down beside a stone wall, getting stonier underfoot as we head for the ruin seen at the start of our walk. We come down to a corner of the stone walled field (sic) to take a path which comes down onto a clearer trail which follows a small stony valley. Our path widens to a track passing a path on our left as the valley flattens out and our car comes into view ahead as we join the route of Walk 3 to come back onto the pavement beside our start point (112M) at the end of our compact adventure.

We like coastal walks, whether they be on promenades for easy strolling or out along wild coastlines such as Walk 11 Peña del Rubicon and Walk 24 A Path Between Two Seas. Here we have a logical extension to our range of walking routes around **Costa Teguise**, as we follow the coastal paths from **Los Cocoteros** to the outskirts of **Costa Teguise**. On the maps it looks like a flat stroll, but there are more than enough sharp ups and downs, which combined with the distance, easily justify a 3 walker rating. This pristine, wild coastline is exposed to the elements so cover up against the sun and take plenty of drinking water.

Los Cocoteros is an unusual settlement of largely holiday homes, meaning it's quiet in the week but can be busy at weekends and *fiestas* when their owners take a break from city life in **Arrecife** to decamp to the coast. It's way off the tourist track and as the Lanzaroteans usually bring all their supplies with them, there are no tourist facilities such as cafés and bars.

If you are staying in **Costa Teguise** then you might consider walking our route in reverse, then having an ocean-side picnic lunch (take it with you) in **Los Cocoteros** before returning along the coastal paths.

Access by car:
On the LZ-1 from **Tahiche** we take the **Guatiza** exit at the 11km marker to come onto the old main road, now the LZ-404. At the first houses of **Guatiza** we take the first street on our right, following it through the town's outskirts to overlook the coastal plain, from where it's gently downhill, following the road through a sharp left turn marked by a waypost to reach the south of **Los Cocoteros**. There's plenty of roadside parking opposite the first of the village houses; however, it can be busy at weekends and *fiestas*, when you might consider following the broad dirt road ahead instead of taking the sharp left turn at the waypost, to follow the dirt road across to the parking area adjacent to Wp.2.

We start on the chrome-railed walkway (Wp.1 0M) alongside the road to walk round the seaward side of the houses to take a well-walked trail heading towards the salt pans where we find a boat ramp (Wp.2 4M) and parking area, our alternative start when **Los Cocoteros** is busy.

There's a myriad of trails so we simply choose one heading (SW) towards houses built above **Playa del Tío Joaquín**. First, we pass a fort-like hut at the edge of old salt pans before joining a dirt track, leaving it as it sweeps inland, as we follow a walking trail along the foreshore.

Alongside the old salt pans

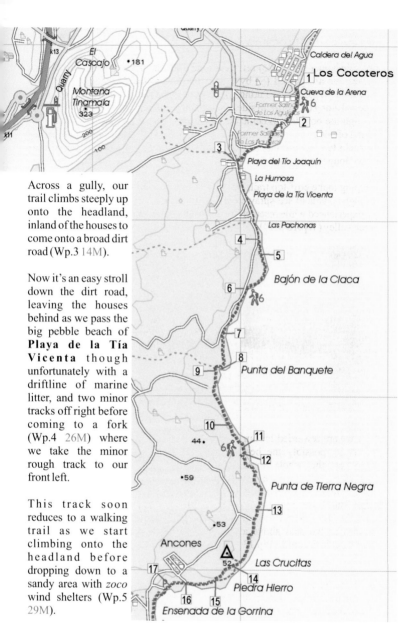

Across a gully, our trail climbs steeply up onto the headland, inland of the houses to come onto a broad dirt road (Wp.3 14M).

Now it's an easy stroll down the dirt road, leaving the houses behind as we pass the big pebble beach of **Playa de la Tía Vicenta** though unfortunately with a driftline of marine litter, and two minor tracks off right before coming to a fork (Wp.4 26M) where we take the minor rough track to our front left.

This track soon reduces to a walking trail as we start climbing onto the headland before dropping down to a sandy area with *zoco* wind shelters (Wp.5 29M).

Our onward trail runs on the seaward side of concrete marker posts to take us along the coastline before dropping down into a shallow valley.

From the valley, our trail climbs up to the top of cliffs to join a dirt track (Wp.6 36M), the same dirt track we left at Wp.4. After eighty metres on the track, we leave it again as it swings right while we continue on a narrow, cairn-marked trail above lava slopes that run down to the sea. We come back to the track again for a few metres before it takes us down into a shallow valley marked by a large *zoco* wind shelter (Wp.7 42M).

Our climb out of the valley brings us onto a headland where our trail becomes fainter; we are guided (S) by cairns to come above the mouth of a small *barranco* (Wp.8 48M). Taking what might loosely be described as a trail, we descend along the northern side of the cleft by picking a line of least resistance through the boulders to come down onto the *barranco*'s pebble beach, just inland of which is a small lagoon. Facing south-west, we clamber up through the rocks to find ourselves on a walking trail (Wp.9 52M) that has taken a long inland loop to cross the *barranco*.

Keeping to the cliff-top trail, we ignore branches towards the sea as we walk through an area of sea-spray covered cliffs, caused by the stiff onshore wind we experienced while researching this route, before coming down into a lava-block valley (Wp.10 61M).

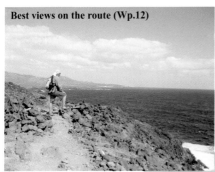

Best views on the route (Wp.12)

Now a steady ascent brings us up around the head of the cliffs, to the view of yet more cliffs ahead. Now it is a picky descent down to a sandy valley floor (Wp.11 65M) followed by another steady climb up to the top of the cliffs again.

Cairn art?

Now we are rewarded for our efforts by possibly the best views on the whole route (Wp.12 67M). For once, we can now make steady progress along the cliffs (SE & S) without too many sharp inclines as we pass above a sharp inlet in the cliffs (Wp.13 75M).

As we get closer to **Costa Teguise** and the settlement of **Ancones** we start to see a plethora of possible trails. In these potentially confusing conditions, our rule is to take the main trail heading (S to SW) towards the resort; most of the trail splits rejoin again shortly after the split.

A hundred metres after a cairned trail leads off towards the 52 metre peak our trail has a major split (Wp.14 84M) where we take the inland right hand option; you could take the seaward left hand option but it involves more ups and downs before rejoining three hundred metres later (Wp.15 89M). The desert settlement of **Ancones** is away on our right, while our trail takes us down into a valley littered with lava blocks directly below the settlement's houses where we come onto a track running up the valley to **Ancones**.

At a junction we take a walking trail left to another track that leads to one of the surprises of this route. We've been walking through wild untamed landscapes, of which this valley is typical so it is a surprise to happen upon a neatly built lava block wall that edges wide lava laid steps heading down to the sea (Wp.16 93M). At the next path junction we take the inland option and go straight over the next path crossroads which brings us to a steep, picky descent to a parking area next to the sea (Wp.17 96M).

We take the walking trail's continuation from the parking area, another option is to take the dirt track accessing the parking area, ignoring a minor path a little later as we head (S) directly towards the resort and come onto the dirt track (Wp.18 104M) that serves **Ancones**. Now it is simply striding out along the broad dirt road until we meet the 'red' circular route (Wp.19 112M) to come onto the end of the promenade. Along the promenade we pass the **Sands Beach Resort** and then cut across a large car park (Wp.20 119M) to the **Avenida de las Islas Canarias** (Wp.21 121M) a few metres east of a taxi rank.

While this is our official finish, where you stop depends upon your plans. For refreshments, you could stay on the promenade to indulge in the Brit and Irish bars facing **Playa Cucharas**, though our choice would be to continue west on **Avenida de las Islas Canarias** to the choice of cafés behind **Centro Comercial Las Cucharas** or **Helga's Kitchen** off the western end of the car parking.

Playa Blanca is Lanzarote's newest and showiest resort, but it is a resort of two halves, so for our first exploration we will test out the affluent western promenade. It's easy strolling on a paved promenade, although it would seriously benefit from a *tipico* bar at its end on the edge of the **Rubicón** desert.

Access by bus:
Take bus N°60 from **Arrecife** to **Playa Blanca** or N°61 **Puerto del Carmen** to **Playa Blanca**, alight at the port bus stop, and walk down to the blue bar on the right where the coastal promenade starts.

Access by car:
Park either opposite **Centro Commercial Limones** or around the port area.

Extension

After the tourist commercialisation of the western promenade our route finishes in near perfect isolation - perfect, that is, if it had a cliff-top bar. If you wish to explore further then we suggest following the route of Walk 11 to waypoint 6 where we turn right (E) to follow the street through **Faro Park**, where there is a possibility of refreshments, and out onto the dual carriageway to the first roundabout with options A & B.

    A: Going right, we follow the street to take the access lane to the *faro* where we rejoin our outward route.

    B: Go straight over the roundabout; at the start of **Playa Bogardo** on our left, we go right on the access street to **Kamezi**. At the end of the street we walk round the western edge of the complex to come back onto the promenade near waypoint 8.

We start on the promenade (Wp.1 0M) to walk alongside bars on the commercial centre's seaward side, now displaying a much smarter appearance than in the days before the promenade opened. The port slips behind us as the brick-paved walkway runs along the top of cliffs and curves right around the **Lanzarote Park Hotel** (Wp.2) and comes down to the beach and bars in front of **Playa Flamingo**. From the end of the beach we climb up to a viewpoint (Wp.3 15M) manufactured out of an old gun pit.

After the small climb it's up and down past the **Timanfaya Palace Hotel**, and its mini-beach, then past the new development of **Playa Real**, to stroll past the seaward visage of the **Natura Palace Hotel**, at the end of which is a walkway (Wp.4 28M) leading up to the road serving the hotel, an alternative return route on pavements. A cute wooden bridge (Wp.5) takes us over a water runoff to start passing the extensive grounds of the **Rubicón Palace Hotel**, almost a town in itself, if the size of its jacuzzi (Wp.6) is anything to go by. By comparison, the seaward face of the **Hotel Club Calimera**

Montaña Roja stands out ahead

(Wp.7) is a fussy collection of little *zocos* and tiny beaches festooned with 'hotel residents only' signs.

Putting the fussiness behind us, we pass another hotel before reaching the artificial beach of **Playa Familia** in front of **Villas Kamezi**, where the promenade finishes at the end of the villa development (Wp.8 44M) - well, that's where it finished when our first edition was published, but now the coastal promenade has been extended to take in the proposed new developments.

As with many areas of **Playa Blanca** the money ran out leaving an extended promenade heading towards the *faro*, still looking pretty fresh after its recent repainting. Strolling along this final section, we have views over the start of the **Rubicón** desert which has proved as tricky as quicksand for property developers' dreams of massive profits. We traverse the edge of the desert in Walk 11, taking in that crumbling monument to the foolishness of pursuing mammon in this desert, **Atlante del Sol**. If only that lesson had been learnt, the desecration caused by further failed developments might have been avoided.

The *faro*

Now, if only someone had built a cliff-top bar at the end of the extended promenade, it would be the perfect easy stroll; failing such luxuries we return by retracing our outward route along the promenade and back to the port, refreshments and bus services.

Now completed, **Playa Blanca**'s eastern promenade offers comfortable strolling between the resort centre and **Playa del Afe**. There's plenty of seating along the way, the cliff-top seating overlooking **Playa del Afe** being notable, but refreshment opportunities are few once outside the resort centre.

If arriving by bus and intending to head out to **Papagayo** on Walk 10, you can use this route to reach the alternative start of the route.

Our choice is to drive to **Playa del Afe** and walk into **Playa Blanca** 'old town'. That way, your refreshment opportunities are improving all the time, and you have the option of a taxi back to your start if you don't feel like walking; starting out from the 'old town' offers the exact opposite!

Access by bus:
If not staying in **Playa Blanca**, take the Nº60 or 61 bus and alight at the second roundabout and walk down the road to a third roundabout, where walkways go down to link to the coastal promenade. Your route is as described below but in reverse. There's also the option of using the town's own circular bus Nº30 which leaves from **Playa Blanca** bus station to access the east of the town, thus walking into the old town as described.

Access by car:
Follow the road down through the third roundabout and head west. After going straight across three roundabouts take the next road right, go straight over two roundabouts onto the cul-de-sac serving **Playa del Afe** and our start is 150 metres away eastwards.

The eastern promenade finishes at the **Playa del Afe** (Wp.1 0M), a once-popular cozzie-optional pebble beach before development arrived. Note that, although the 'Playa Papagayo' blue sign points inland, the traditional walking route to this beautiful beach is along the **Playa del Afe** promenade to paths leading up the headland on the seaward side of the **Papagayo Arena Hotel**.

From the eastern end of **Playa del Afe** we take the promenade away from the beach to head uphill then a little dink left and a dink right sees us walking up past the seaward side of the **Iberostar Papagayo Hotel** to the cul-de-sac on our right (Wp.2) to come onto the plateau above the cliffs.

It's now easy strolling along the broad path to a junction (Wp.3) with **Castillo Coloradas** access and a road on our right where our view is held by the lava mountain, or 'slag heap', of the **Volcán Lanzarote Hotel**

Views from the promenade

The Rubicón Marina

Continuing on the path past houses, we come to a *mirador* viewpoint overlooking the **Rubicón Marina** (Wp.4 19M). Down the steps (right), or slopes (left), we have a choice of following the paved walkway (our GPS track), or making our way through the marina's bustling commercial centre.

Keeping to the walkway we pass the front of the **Volcán Lanzarote Hotel** plus some unoccupied premises before reaching a bar/restaurant (Wp.5) - important as it is the last refreshment opportunity if walking out from the resort - before we cross the marina's access road to come back onto seafront promenade (Wp.6) to continue alongside the lava foreshore, passing a house engulfed in trees (Wp.7) before coming back to hotel developments.

The promenade twists down to pass **Playa Coloradas** beach (Wp.8) and then climbs to bring the 'old town' into view. For the final stage, we are squeezed between bars and the sea, passing stairways up to the main road should you wish to escape at any time. Keeping straight ahead on the promenade we finally leave the bars behind as we come to overlook the port and the paved walkway swings right to take us up to the road (Wp.9 60M).

197 metres might not sound like much of a mountain, but located where it is in the flat deserts of **Playa Blanca**, this counts as a high summit. Easy way-finding on well marked paths with enough of a climb for a sense of achievement, this is a popular ascent, perhaps because it is such a contrast to the featureless resort development. A route for all ages; we were accompanied by a three year old boy and his parents on our latest visit.

| 3 | H | 3 km | 150m 150m | ↻ | 0 |

Short Walk option - this *is* the short walk.

Access by bus:
N°60 from **Arrecife** or N°61 via **Puerto del Carmen** to **Playa Blanca** bus station, from where there are two choices. Either walk inland (N) along the main road to pass the CEPSA petrol station and go left (W) at the roundabout, strolling along the **Avenida Faro Pechiguera** pavement to the third roundabout where we go right on **Calle Francia** (N) to come gently uphill to **Paradise Island Club**,where we turn left (W) onto **Avenida Noruega** to our official start at Wp.1. Adds 2½ km to the route.

Alternatively, take the N°30 **Playa Blanca** town bus from the town's bus station (a rather roundabout route) to **Virginia Park** which is 2 stops after the school (Colegio). Walk south towards the sea for a few metres, then first right is **Avenida Noruega.**

Access by car:
If you are driving, we suggest parking at the outer fringes of the development.

At last we are heading for the mountain, passing **Los Clavelles** on our left as we head uphill to the road junction alongside **Montaña Baja** development; drivers should park on the road in this general area.

A giant pebble points the way

The 'Al Volcan' sign (Wp.1 0M) points us up the road, to a street junction (Wp.2). Development scourge has meant that the old start to the path has been cut off by an abandoned development so we walk up the street to the end of the fence where the path now starts.

It's a dusty sloping path that winds its way up towards the ridge, passing a path coming from the left (Wp.3, and an alternative start route) and bringing us onto the broad back of the ridge (Wp.4 15M) to meet a dirt road coming in from the north.

Our ascent of Montaña Roja lies ahead.

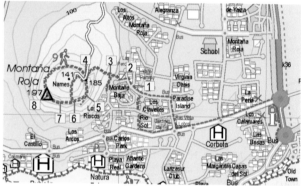

Stone names decorate the floor of the *caldera*.

Our choice is to go left to circle the crater clockwise, gently uphill overlooking a large array of 'stone names' which have been laid out on the floor of the *caldera*.

Following our ascent, we now have an easy stroll with views over the new hotels to **Papagayo**. At a path junction (Wp.5) we have an optional peak to visit on our left, or can go down to a saddle (Wp.6) where a path descends into the *caldera*, an optional steep short cut. Continuing round the crater rim, we have a climbing section alongside lichen-covered rocks to a saddle viewpoint (Wp.7) and then a moderately serious ascent up to the trig point (Wp.8 27M).

After the trig point we pass another saddle viewpoint, after which our trail descends, curving right and flattening out for an easy stroll along to the dirt track into the *caldera*. Now it is gently up to meet our upward path (Wp.4 40M) on the wide ridge, and back down the dusty trail to our car - or if using the bus, a longer stroll back into the resort or to await the town bus N°30 back to the bus station.

10 PAPAGAYO BEACH

Playa de Papagayo is one of the most photographed locations on Lanzarote and in our view, is the one that lives up to its image when you arrive there. The easy option is to drive there, following the road signs onto the dirt roads on the southern **Rubicón Plain**, pay your 'gate' fee and park in the extensive parking area near the bars; you are then left with only the steep descent to, and ascent from, this cliff-enclosed perfect beach.

The easy 'car' option is eschewed by aficionados like us, who feel that the beauty of the beaches in this isolated region is enhanced by expending a bit of effort in gaining the reward. **Playas Mujeres** and **Pozo**, which we cross on the way to **Papagayo**, and **Playa Congrio** are also beautiful beaches with the added attraction of being cozzie-optional. So to make a day of it, take your cozzie - or not, as the mood takes you - and enjoy some of the best beaches on the island, their beauty enhanced by the barren surroundings in which they are found.

Access by bus:
Alight from the Nº60 or Nº61 bus at the roundabout after the petrol station, and walk down into the 'old town' to join the Extended Walk.

Access by car:
On the LZ2, go straight over the petrol station roundabout and the next roundabout to a third roundabout at the edge of the old town. Here, go left (there is no other way) to head east on **Avenida Papagayo**, keeping on the main road until you encounter blue (walker) **Playa Papagayo** signs; yellow signs will direct on the dirt road and 'gate' route for drivers. When you see the sign directing walkers onto a cinder track, blocked to vehicle access by large boulders, look for an on-street parking place on the road up to the **Papagayo Arena Hotel**.

Short Walk
To **Playa Mujeres** and return.

Extended Walk
Take Walk 8, Coastal Promenade - Playa Blanca East f rom the 'old town' to the start of this route and return the same way. When you reach the end of the last stretch of coastal promenade blue signs direct you inland to our official start point, but you could cross the shingle beach to paths that climb up the headland on the hotel's seaward side; see map section.

So many people have walked this route over the years, in all its possible forms, that we have literally a confusion of tracks and trails, most of which will eventually lead you to **Papagayo**; for a description we could simply say "Go east into the wilderness, and stop when you find paradise", but you probably expect a bit more than that.

For GPS users, loading up our waypoints will be a great help. For those without the benefit of satellite technology, do follow our outward route; it may not always be the best, but it's the way we arrived at paradise.

Signs point the way at Wp.1

We start out from the street below the **Papagayo Arena Hotel** where a blue 'Playa Papagayo' sign (Wp.1 0M) directs us up a cinder track.

Past the boulders barring vehicle access, we climb up to a junction (Wp.2) behind the hotel and take the faint track to the left to come up onto a featureless desert plateau - featureless except for the pointless trig point on our front left that supposedly marks the peak of **Papagayo**, but do not be drawn towards it.

Keeping to the faint track we come up a rise that brings the beaches into view, car windscreens acting like mirrors in the large car parks as our route curves right past a cairn to a faint junction (Wp.3) where we keep straight on towards the distant car park. Strolling over the headland, we have various trails on our right as we come to the top of a steep trail (Wp.4) which gives us a skittery descent down to the back of **Playa Mujeres (**Wp.5 16M) beside the first car park.

Walking across the rear of the beach behind the dunes, we pass the second car park (Wp.6) to a choice of a steep sandy path which runs up from the beach, or we can continue ahead up a sandy *barranco*, followed by an open-ground ascent over rock onto the next headland - our choice.

Cairns provide approximate direction markers to the start of a path (Wp.7) dropping down to **Playa del Pozo**, the path finishing in a small rock scramble to drop us onto the beach (Wp.8 30M). Straight across the beach, we head for a path (Wp.9) climbing the sloping rock face onto the next headland.

Papagayo beach

We climb up the path, the sand changing to purple rock as we come onto the headland, the car park now much closer as we cross a water-eroded gully (Wp.10) followed by an ascent, and crossing a second gully before coming up to the bars above **Papagayo** beach (Wp.11 45M).

Past the bar's generator, a manicured walkway is signed to the beach taking us between the bars. There's a choice of three bars for refreshments and, given their spectacularly isolated position, prices are very reasonable; regard a refreshment stop on their terrace as compulsory, and enjoy the views down onto Lanzarote's best beach.

If you are planning on sunbathing, take one of the steep paths which lead down to the perfect beach, though take care on their slippery surfaces, and it will be (of course) an equally steep climb back up.

Playa Mujeres behind us on the return

For our return we chose an inland wandering route from the car park, crossing those gullies higher up (much easier to cross) and taking in the wooden cross (Wp.12) and line of boulders before meeting the access track to **Playa Mujeres** at its junction (Wp.13) before rejoining our outward route at Wp.5.

There are so many tracks and trails through this desert landscape that you could navigate back by simply heading north and avoiding any pitfalls. If you do not have a compass or GPS, then use the trig point pillar as your general direction marker.

"Deserts have a strange unreality all of their own. Driving across the **Rubicón** desert, there's a sense that nothing has happened here in aeons; walking there gives an even greater sense of timelessness - it's easy to imagine that whole civilisations might have disappeared under the wastes of the world's great deserts. Our excursion is along the seaward margin of the **Rubicón**, passing some beautiful rock pools set in the lava foreshore, to the *peña* of this desert, the long-abandoned **Atlante del Sol Hotel**, a monument to the foolishness of investing in the desert." That was our original summary. The foolishness of property developer greed is evident in **Playa Blanca**'s recently abandoned developments, yet the **Atlante del Sol**'s dramatic isolation still stands as a monument to the failure of 'desert dreams' decades after its ill-fated construction.

Originally a 'there & back' walk, we've now extended it into a linear route taking in the desalination plant and **Las Salinas** salt pans before arriving at **La Hoya** to catch the bus back to **Playa Blanca**. An adventurous but easy route skirting the dramatic lava cliff coast between the wild Atlantic (on our left) and the **Rubicon** desert (on our right), it has a wilderness feel all the way until we overlook **Las Salinas**. Sun protection and plenty of drinking water are essential, especially in the summer months. It's best to do this route on a weekday as buses calling at **Rotónda La Hoya** are rare on Sundays/holidays.

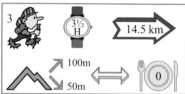

Shorter Option
To **Atlante del Sol** and return to the *faro* (11km, 3 hours).

Access by bus:
Bus Nº60 or 61 to the port in **Playa Blanca** and follow our western coastal promenade route (Walk 7) to its end where Wp.8 of that route becomes Wp.1 of this route; add 1 hour to your total time. Bus Nº60 stops at **Rotónda La Hoya** on both its inward and outward journeys between **Arrecife** and **Playa Blanca**; see appendices at the back of this book for timetables.

Access by car: 2CSK Route (see P.17)
Given that this is a long linear route, you might consider parking near the main bus stop in **Playa Blanca** and following Walk 7 to our official start - see Access by Bus - add one hour to our walking time.

Our start point is the western end of the coastal

promenade (Wp.1 0M) where we step round the end of **Villas Kamezi** and cross open ground to come onto the remains of a tarmac road. At the end of the tarmac we go left on the dirt base of a new road, and then right on a smaller track to come to the twin light houses of **Faro de Pechiguera**, one small and squat and one tall and imperious, (Wp.2 11M). We work our way round the lighthouses to leave on a small path beside a low wall (Wp.3) which widens to a track which brings us up to a turning circle by the **Finistere** development (Wp.4 16M). Now we have the luxury of a promenade, but it doesn't last long and we are back on dirt track and trail until we climb over a boulder mound to come onto another turning circle (Wp.5 20M). Now we're back on a better financed promenade, strolling between foaming foreshore and lifeless houses before coming to the access into **Faro Park** development (Wp.6 28M).

Shortly, in 190 metres, the promenade finishes along with the houses, and we have a scruffy little section before coming onto a track, then taking a minor track ahead when the main track swings right, to cross a water runoff and come to a junction (Wp.7 40M) where a track goes right to the tarmac access road. Continuing ahead, we pass an isolated house on its seaward side, the track ending for us to negotiate the end of the property's wall and a runoff before coming onto a trail paralleling the coast. Our trail widens to a track and views open up over the nothingness of the **Rubicón** desert as we head for another isolated house, recognisably scruffy even at this distance.

As we close with the scruffy house, getting even scruffier as we close with it, the monstrous ugliness that is the **Atlante del Sol** comes into view. Approaching the house (Wp.8 50M), we find a motley collection of caravans and vans seemingly attached to it, and a street name 'Cala Malva 1', obviously owned by an optimist still awaiting the arrival of **Playa Blanca**'s outskirts.

As is the way of deserts, it's a surprise to find ugliness or nothingness, standing alongside something of great beauty - think of those **Papagayo** beaches backed by featureless, barren desert. It's the case here as, opposite the house, metal steps lead down the cliffs to a exciting lava foreshore containing beautiful rock pools. From the house we continue along the track running above the cliffs, a branch going out onto a 'table' headland (Wp.9), the track becoming sandy as we pass a small lava peak (Wp.10), just after which is a bulldozed area where rocks have been heaped up and also a lava rock wall which serves no obvious purpose. It's almost as if we've passed into an illogical unreality as our track goes left in front of the wall while we go left on a trace of a track which soon peters out among the lava-topped cliffs. Ahead, our destination of **Atlante del Sol** seems close as we come inland to seek a route amongst the tracery of faint tracks and trails which dissect the rock-

littered sandy desert. We weave our way across the plain, passing a walled farm on our right to come upon the unexpected sight of a swampy lagoon in front of the fire-darkened shell of the hotel.

Signs of 'occupation' at the abandoned hotel

Skirting the noisome waters, we pass on the seaward side of the first wing and walk across the open ground to the far wing (Wp.11 78M) where we happen upon signs of occupation in the form of beds and a kitchen set up amongst the ground floor rooms; not our choice of 'weekender' accommodation in the shadow of the hotel's brooding ugliness, but then it takes all sorts!

'*Peña*' is strange Spanish word which doesn't translate well into English. The best we can offer is 'punishment' or 'inner pain', or 'torment', as when deciding between two unpleasant options. Standing by this financial and physical ruin that once was someone's expected boom town, the power of the desert and the ability of its nothingness to absorb even the best laid plans and investments is palpable.

Of course there are now far bigger monuments to developers' greed littering the southern edge of the desert, but it's a chilling thought that **Atlante del Sol** has stood abandoned for over three decades. How long will it be before the abandoned developments of **Playa Blanca** finally disappear?

Samari

unta de Piedra Alta

la del Convento

Rincón del Palo

Punta Gorda **Atlante del Sol**

La Piedra de los Femés

Punta Ginés

Our original route, now our Shorter Option, is to return from here to the *faro*, but today we're off across the desert heading for **Las Salinas** and the **La Hoya** bus stop to catch a ride back to **Playa Blanca**.

From the hotel's northern corner (0M) we walk out over the open ground (approx. E) to come onto a faint track, just slightly more cleared than the surrounding desert, which curves away from the sea (E) and gradually becomes more track-like as we come into onto a well-used track (Wp.12 8M).

That's the difficult navigation over as we turn left to follow the rough track (don't even think of bringing your hire car here) as it heads towards the coastline (NE). It's easy strolling along the undulating track which flattens as we progress, and splits for a short section before passing a *zoco* style wind shelter (Wp.13

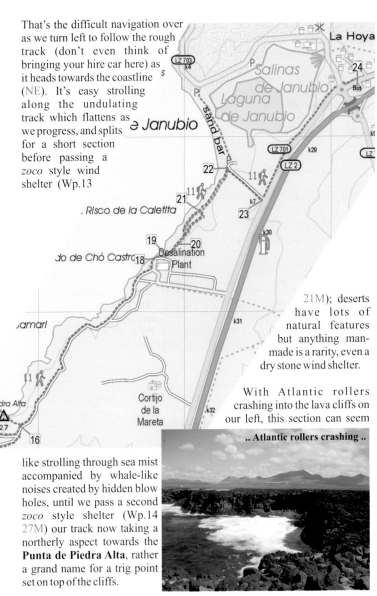

21M); deserts have lots of natural features but anything man-made is a rarity, even a dry stone wind shelter.

With Atlantic rollers crashing into the lava cliffs on our left, this section can seem

.. Atlantic rollers crashing ..

like strolling through sea mist accompanied by whale-like noises created by hidden blow holes, until we pass a second *zoco* style shelter (Wp.14 27M) our track now taking a northerly aspect towards the **Punta de Piedra Alta**, rather a grand name for a trig point set on top of the cliffs.

Just after our track divides (Wp.15 35M), you might like to walk over to the cliffs to see rock-climbing fittings that allow cliff mountaineers to absaill down to the lava-shelf foreshore by the **El Convento** cave; most impressive if you happen to see them in use. Black cubist rocks decorate the cliff top plateau on the section before we come opposite the trig point (Wp.16 42M) to walk across the open ground and from beside the trig point (Wp.17) we have a superb view of lava shelf foreshore and sea-delved cave with the Atlantic rollers crashing over the shelf in a foaming mass, one of the most spectacular sea views on the island. Back on our track, we head for the desalination plant directly ahead, after a particularly rough section the track smooths out for us to make easy progress. As we close on the plant the track divides, the right hand track is clearer but both sections will lead us up to the parking area from where we walk up to the northern face of the plant (Wp.18 74M).

Atlante del Sol to the desalination plant (5km) has been easy walking, but looking north towards **Las Salinas**, we now face a broken landscape as the desert runs out. Despite first appearances, it is an easy section only requiring more concentration on where we're putting our feet as we stroll across (NE) to a track junction (Wp.19) where we keep ahead (NE) on a degraded rough rock track overlooking a small disused quarry; if you take the left fork at Wp.19 you'll be walking across the floor of the quarry to its wall of tumbled rocks where a cairn marked path climbs up to join our main route (Wp.20).

On the narrow trail towards Las Salinas

We stay on the rough track; in 120 metres a path goes down to our front left. We can either stay on the higher rough track or take the lower trail, both options rejoining 280 metres later (Wp.21) after the high route has come onto a better track which runs out at this point.

Ahead of us (NE) is the welcome sight of a narrow walking trail snaking up and down, in and out, of the tumbled landscape. After all that walking on desert tracks it's very satisfying to be on a trail that's the only choice of route. We wind our way towards the small car park above the **Las Salinas** sand bar. As we close with the car park there are higher and lower options which come together again as we step off the trail at the bottom of the dirt road access from the LZ701 (Wp.22 97M).

Below us, trails lead down onto the sand bar that protects the **Las Salinas** salt pans from the fury of the Atlantic, and across the bar to another car park on the far side. The bar runs down to an exciting beach but on no account should you be tempted to swim here as the currents can be treacherous. Across the salt pans is the inviting sight of a bar/restaurant that isn't on our route but you could be tempted into a diversion if the bus timetable allows.

It's been an interesting route so far and it would be good to say that the excitement lasts right up to the end but sadly, we're now into the boring piece of getting to the bus stop. You could try cutting across the hills up to the road but more straightforward is an uphill slog to the LZ701 road (Wp.23 105M), then turn north to walk along the road to the roundabout – be careful as although this is a quiet road, what traffic there is whizzes along as though its trying to outpace vehicles on the LZ2 main road. Across the roundabout, it's just 180 metres to the **La Hoya** bus stop and shelter (Wp.24 123M). If your timing and the bus schedule allows it is an easy stroll down from the roundabout to the bar/restaurant picturesquely situated overlooking the salt pans but allow a good fifteen minutes uphill return in time to catch your bus back to **Playa Blanca**.

To commemorate the devastating volcanic eruptions of 1730-1736, in which the **Yaiza** region suffered the worst depredations, the local government built an elevated walkway and gardens running around the base of **Montaña Cinta**. This makes for easy strolling combined with views over the town to the lava sea and **Timanfaya**.

Unfortunately, they forgot to complete the centre section of the walkway, thus requiring us to do a little traditional path walking to join the two sections. They also forgot to tell anyone that these gardens exist, so although tour buses park near our start, you are likely to have the **Volcanic Gardens** and their views to yourself.

Our Walk 13 Yaiza - Las Breñas Circular offers a more challenging route which also takes in the gardens.

Access by bus:
The Nº60 takes you into **Yaiza**.

Access by car:
Park off the old main road through **Yaiza** behind the church, where there is plenty of on-street parking and an official car park in front of the police station.

> **Short Walk**
> This is a short walk, but you can shorten it further by taking the stair access down to the old main road opposite **El Campo Bar/Restaurant**.

We start out from the church (Wp.1 0M) to walk south past government administration buildings (note the 'Educación, Cultura y Festivos' office on the left, where you may be able to pick up their 'Ruta de Cabellos' leaflet) to a multi-street junction with a confusion of traffic arrows painted on the roadway.

... views over Yaiza ...

On our front right is a lava wall containing planted gardens and a wide rock stairway, which we climb to come onto a broad red cinder track (Wp.2). The most energetic section of the route is already completed, as we turn right to stroll along the elevated walkway taking in the views over **Yaiza** town.

Our stroll curves around the hillside to the end of the first section of gardens (Wp.3), the second section of gardens facing us across a valley as we continue on a dirt track along the southern side of the valley. The fields on the valley floor are edged with earth mounds, and at the end of the second large field (Wp.4 10M) the track continues ahead while we go right onto a path which runs along the top of an earth mound (NW).

At the northern side of the field we swing right, dropping down to cross a gully between the mounds, and then left (NW) along another mound to come up onto a disused track (Wp.5). Going right, we come down the track, which narrows to a trail after an earth mound to reach the red cinder track at the second section of the 'Volcanic Gardens' (17M).

Views to Montaña Cinta from the path

Aloes along the route

With the cross-country section behind us, it is back to easy strolling as we curve round the mountain to come above the **El Campo Bar/Rest**, where an access stairway drops down to the road (Wp.6); our Short Walk option.

Both sections of the **Volcanic Gardens** have been well planted; the Aloe plants and Euphorbia varieties that line the track are particularly fine specimens, so it's a great disappointment when this planting runs out and the final section resembles a scene of crucifixion rather than a garden, with young saplings staked out to die without water on the barren slopes.

At the end of this depressing section a dirt track continues round the mountain to **La Finca**, while we go right (Wp.7 25M) down a steep track that drops us down to the access road for the outlying houses of **Yaiza**. Once on the access track, we head right towards the old main road and **El Campo**, passing some scruffy houses before reaching the main road where we choose to take a refreshment stop in **El Campo Bar/Rest.** (Wp.8 30M). Our return is to simply walk along the pavement, up to our starting point at the church.

With the rash of wayposts planted by the authorities you might think they've got all the interesting walking covered - far from it, as we discover a beautiful airy walk that combines natural landscapes, thought-provoking art, and gastronomy in a route that nobody else seems to have discovered. Starting in **Yaiza**, we take an unlikely and rather unappealing exit from the town to reach the saddle below **Atalaya de Femés**, where we step out on a narrow donkey trail with elevated views. When the trail ends we have a modicum of road walking, enlivened by the house of a famous artist with its unusual alfresco artworks, followed by lunch at our favourite Lanzarote *tipico*. Post refreshment, we leave **Las Breñas** to cross the *malpais* on bits and pieces of old jeep tracks and open ground walking to reach our final section where our gently elevated route gives us a new aspect over the lava fields and **Yaiza**.

In a nutshell it's a route that has just about everything you could hope for and at a low exertion rating. Note that **Casa Marcos** and **El Restinga** bar/restaurants in **Las Breñas** both close on Mondays. At 16kms might seem a bit long for a relaxed walk; our advice is to taxi from **Yaiza** to **La Degollada** which saves 3.2kms and the main ascent of 140 metres altitude.

*just 60 metres of ascents after **La Degollada**
Casa Marcos and **El Restinga** are closed Mondays

Access by car:
From the the LZ-2 take the roundabout exit for **Yaiza** and take the old main road into town. From the roundabout drive to **Yaiza** church, 1.8km from the south or 0.8km from the east, then turn south to park near the *ayuntamiento* offices and start of Walk 12 Yaiza Gardens. Usually there's a local taxi (deep red Mercedes estate) parked here for a ride up to **La Degollada**.

From the old main road (Wp.1 0M) we walk south, the church on our left and *ayuntamiento* offices on our right to the start of our Walk 12 Yaiza Gardens route (Wp.2) where Walk 14 Atalaya de Femés Linear heads left (ESE) towards the main mountain. Our route is straight ahead (S then SW) on the main lane heading for **La Degollada**. There's not a lot to say about this section, a tarmac lane with little traffic, rising gently - surroundings a bit dull. Then it steepens quite dramatically as we approach the settlement.

On the dirt track at Wp.3

We find ourselves in a 'huff and puff' steep tarmac ascent between the first and rather cute white houses with green detailing set amongst lava-walled cultivated black *picon* plots. Finally we come to the top of the lane to find ourselves on the saddle between the **Atalaya de Femés** and **Montaña El Cabo** (Wp.3 60M) - by this point you'll probably appreciate our suggestion of taking the **Yaiza** taxi to this location at the end of the tarmac. From the end of the tarmac, we continue on a dirt track that in fifty metres has shrunk to a narrow walking trail that contours (SW) along the hillside below the **Atalaya de Femés**. While our trail is narrow it is comfortable walking with superb views over the **Janubio** lagoon and **Las Breñas** village from our elevated 300+ metres altitude. After climbing gently our path comes under lichen-covered lava boulders stacked dramatically above our route (Wp.4 72M), giving the impression they could avalanche down at any moment - they haven't moved in years, after which the hillside takes on a less dramatic aspect as **Montaña Roja** and **Playa Blanca** come into hazy view across the southern plain.

Since the precarious lava boulders we've been following our contouring trail due south. Now, as the huge quarry at **Maciot Alto** starts to dominate the view, our trail starts dropping (Wp.5 79M), becoming narrower and pickier as our descent increases towards a roofed water reservoir. Carefully picking our way down the narrow trail, almost stepped in parts, we come onto the end of a jeep track and follow this (S) to pass the water reservoir on our right (Wp.6 85M) to come onto the reservoir's access track. It would be useful if a trail cut across to the **Las Breñas** road at this point, but rather than tackle open ground we walk along the access track to the LZ-703 **Las Breñas** road (Wp.7 89M), turn right and stroll down the left hand side, facing the occasional oncoming car, towards **Las Breñas**. We pass a barren football pitch on our left, where a gully is tunneled under the road, before arriving at the village name sign and first house (Wp.8 98M) **Casa de la Cabra Vieja**

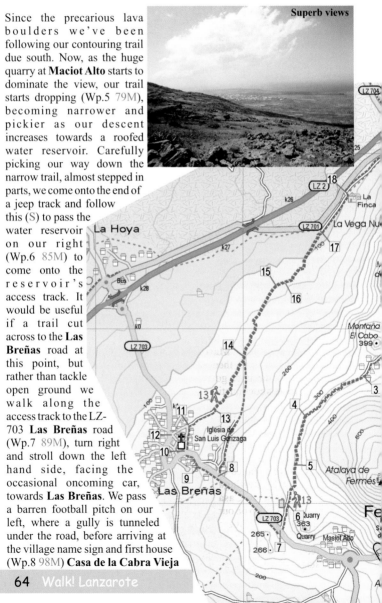

Superb views

- literally 'House of the Old Goat' which possibly might be descriptive or humorous. Opposite, **Calle Las Toscas** - lined with newish villas - goes right off the LZ-703. If you are merely interested in completing this route, then take this street and then the dirt track out to a walled farm after which we will meet you in the *malpais*.

You don't need to be a culture vulture or a gourmand to continue on our main route, though you'll get the opportunity to be both as we continue along the LZ-703 to the unusual sight of a house whose grounds are littered with art, including an oversized trowel dominating the house itself (Wp.9 101M). This is the winter home of Berlin based, internationally renowned, artist Dieter

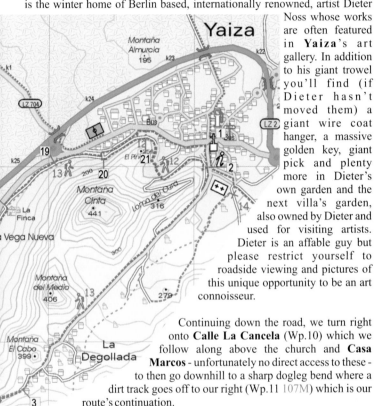

Noss whose works are often featured in **Yaiza**'s art gallery. In addition to his giant trowel you'll find (if Dieter hasn't moved them) a giant wire coat hanger, a massive golden key, giant pick and plenty more in Dieter's own garden and the next villa's garden, also owned by Dieter and used for visiting artists. Dieter is an affable guy but please restrict yourself to roadside viewing and pictures of this unique opportunity to be an art connoisseur.

Continuing down the road, we turn right onto **Calle La Cancela** (Wp.10) which we follow along above the church and **Casa Marcos** - unfortunately no direct access to these - to then go downhill to a sharp dogleg bend where a dirt track goes off to our right (Wp.11 107M) which is our route's continuation.

Our choice is to continue on the street to come along to the main entrance to **Las Breñas** (Wp.12) where, it not being Monday, we have a choice of refreshments at **El Restinga** down on our right or **Casa Marcos** (our choice) up on our left. After refreshment in these laid back *tipicos* we prepare for our return to **Yaiza** in the second stage of our route by

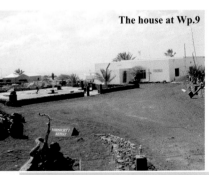

The house at Wp.9

returning to the dirt track on **Calle La Cancela** (Wp.11 0M). Up the track, we come out beside the last of the village houses to overlook the pathless *malpais* which stretches over two kilometres (NE) across to the LZ-701. The *malpais* isn't actually pathless, more a jumble of bits and pieces of old tracks dating back to the

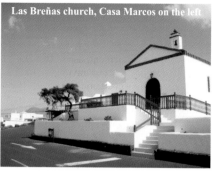

Las Breñas church, Casa Marcos on the left

Leaving Las Breñas

construction of a water pipeline across the plain from the reservoir at Wp.6. At the end of the track we come onto a bit of a trail taking us to an electricity pylon (Wp.13 7M) where we go right to find the surprise of a boulder-laid donkey trail, which unfortunately soon runs out into the *malpais*, after which path finding becomes a bit problematical.

Trying to keep to a NNE heading, we pick our way across a mixture of open ground and the remains of old tracks, taking whichever way seems easiest to gradually make progress across the gently undulating plain. In this mishmash of tracks a white painted stone (Wp.14 15M) helps keep us on track; or rather in the correct direction but effectively 'off track'. From above, the plain looks flat but close up it resolves into a collection of little crests and gullies. We continue NNE until we hit a clearer track (Wp.15 28M) that takes us NE to a piece of abandoned steel pipeline (Wp.16 30M). Then it's over a small crest, followed by the negotiation of a gully as we start closing with the dirt track alongside the LZ-701. The ground is clearer here, for us to clamber down into and out of a dried up watercourse. A short climb brings us up onto the end of a well-stabilised dirt track (Wp.17 36M) and the *malpais* is behind us.

We now have the luxury of a smooth broad track, separated from the road by a sharp obsidian lava 'fence', which climbs gently alongside the LZ-701. Gradually we come up above the roadway for increasing views (W & NW) across the cone dotted lava sea. We cross the access track for the **La Finca** houses (Wp.18) to continue gently ascending until we come to overlook **Yaiza**'s western roundabout (Wp.19 53M); which from hire car level, looks like a large, scrubby roundabout with a few endemic plants resolves itself into an example of road design art when viewed from above. Continuing on the track as it curves around below **Montaña Cinta**, we come to the end of our Walk 12 route (Wp.20 61M) which we follow along to the wide-stepped descent (Wp.21 68M) leading down to the old main road. From here you have a choice of following our Yaiza Gardens route back to Wp.2 or, our choice, descending the steps to cross the road for refreshments in **Restaurante El Campo** before walking up the road back to our start point at Wp.1.

Femés remains our favourite Lanzarote village. While we have the option of driving into the village and ascending the **Atalaya** by our unique circular route, we recognise that bus travellers and classicists like the traditional linear route. This is a long energetic ascent, as after the first kilometre every step is upwards until we reach the antennaed summit, from where we have a choice of returning by the same route to our start point or descending to **Femés**; our preference. Then to return to your start, we suggest our **Atalaya de Femés - Circular Route**, until you meet up with your outward route.

While this is one of the island's wilder routes, wayfinding is very straightforward. Virtually all the route is on clear tracks and paths, and if you do have any navigation questions, the answer is always 'uphill'.

*Distances are **Yaiza/Uga** - **Atalaya** 7 kilometres, **Atalaya** - **Femés** 2.7 kilometres, **Femés** - **Yaiza/Uga** 6.2 kilometres using the 'Circular' route.

> **Stroll**
> V o l c a n i c
> **Gardens** (30 mins, see text).

Access by bus:
Route Nº5 operates a limited **Arrecife - Femés** service Monday to Friday but you'll need to get up early; Nº60 stops at **Yaiza** church on the old main road, or entrance to **Uga**. See appendices at the back of this book for timetables.

Access by car:
2CSK Route (see P.17). Park in the car park near the church in **Yaiza**.

Starting from **Yaiza**.
From outside the church (Wp.1 0M) we walk away from the old main road passing public buildings on each side; note the Cultura y Educación office on the left; to pass a large public square on our left and come to the junction at the top of the square (Wp.2). Ahead the road runs on to **La Degollada**, while on our front right are the **Volcanic Gardens**, built to commemorate the 250th anniversary of the **Timanfaya** eruption.

Stroll
Climbing the many steps, you will come onto a broad walkway which curves around the hillside giving views over **Yaiza** to the **Timanfaya**; surprisingly this gem is little visited by tourists. (See Walk 12, Yaiza's Volcanic Gardens and Walk 13 Yaiza - Las Breñas circular))

From Wp.2, we follow the wide road left (ESE). When the tarmac changes to black *picon* grit (Wp.3), take a break to look up; our eyes are drawn to the massive *lomo* rising up to the **Atalaya** peak, it looks big and distant - both are true, but don't be daunted in your quest. We have easy striding across a plain before the track starts climbing, steadily at first but then steeper as a 'puff and grunt' ascent up to a junction by a giant tooth (Wp.4), once a complete windmill but seemingly more diminished each time we pass.

Starting from Uga

We start from opposite the village road junction; see map. If you get off the bus at the church walk out past **Bar Gregorio** then left, right, left and up to carefully cross the main road.

From the southern side of the junction a dirt road leads up around a large house to a junction where the left hand track is 'Solo Camels'! Keeping left, we come onto a fertile plain after which our track runs along a valley floor as the ridges rise on each side of our route.

Stark farm buildings, including camel farms, line the track until we come to a track off to the right heading toward a huge molar on the ridge above us. We turn up the track to climb up to a saddle and then up the line of the ridge to pass the remains of the old windmill and join our **Yaiza** route (Wp.4).

There's plenty of uphill ahead, so you might want to take a first break on the windmill saddle, with views west across the **Valle de Fena** to the **Volcanic Gardens** and east down over the rather scruffy camel farms, before tackling the serious ascent ahead.

Combined Route

From the 'tooth', our black *picon* track runs straight up the spine in a steady ascent. When the black track goes down towards the **Femés** valley (Wp.5) we keep right on a rocky track, and then keep right at a second cairned track (Wp.6) which leads down into the valley, our return route. We keep right and

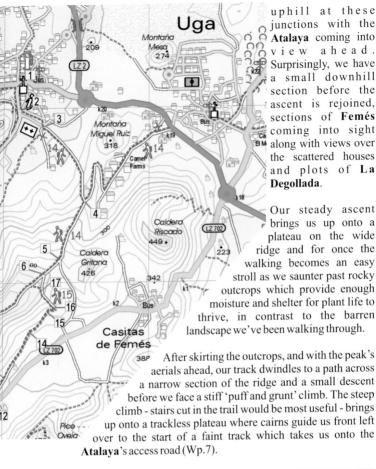

uphill at these junctions with the **Atalaya** coming into view ahead. Surprisingly, we have a small downhill section before the ascent is rejoined, sections of **Femés** coming into sight along with views over the scattered houses and plots of **La Degollada**.

Our steady ascent brings us up onto a plateau on the wide ridge and for once the walking becomes an easy stroll as we saunter past rocky outcrops which provide enough moisture and shelter for plant life to thrive, in contrast to the barren landscape we've been walking through.

After skirting the outcrops, and with the peak's aerials ahead, our track dwindles to a path across a narrow section of the ridge and a small descent before we face a stiff 'puff and grunt' climb. The steep climb - stairs cut in the trail would be most useful - brings up onto a trackless plateau where cairns guide us front left over to the start of a faint track which takes us onto the **Atalaya**'s access road (Wp.7).

Once on the broad dirt road navigation, which has not been at all difficult to this point, becomes simplicity itself. We head up the broad track climbing up through a zigzag to look down into a 'named' *caldera*. It's then a straight uphill slog to the peak's trig point (Wp.8) beside the buildings and aerials.

... the 'named' *caldera* between Wps. 7&8

At the far end of the buildings we find a stepped path leading down to a cave house, just the place to take off your backpack and relax. The two small rooms and plastered walls appear to pre-date the transmitters, and a path leads on to a second smaller cave also shaped for habitation.

Descent to Femés

From the trig point, **Femés** village square looks both inviting and deceptively close. Our descent is so straightforward (we just head down the access track) that no description is necessary except to say, take care. The track is eroded in places and has a loose grit/dust surface in others making for a skittery descent with the possibility of being unceremoniously dumped on your bottom; we know!

On the peak

We pass our upward route (Wp.7 8M) and after a series of zig-zags we pass a track going steeply down to our right (Wp.9). After the chained vehicle barrier (30M) we come onto a village dirt road (Wp.10) to go right and pass the bottom of the track we saw earlier. Reaching the village houses, we come onto tarmac/concrete streets where keeping straight ahead brings us into the village square and **Bar Femés** (Wp.11).

Return to **Yaiza/Uga**

Now, most walkers climb back up the access road to walk back down the ridge to their start point but unless you are a deliberate masochist who enjoys boring uphill climbs, then why not try something a little bit different with the start of our **Atalaya de Femes** - Circular route? It is certainly easier than the access road, and does mean that you are not repeating yourself.

We start out from **Bar Femés** (Wp.11 0M) by walking down the road (NE) away from the village. As the pavement ends (5M) we keep to the main road passing the lower section of the village on our left as easy strolling takes us down past a decorative palm garden before we come to a dirt track (Wp.12, 19M). We take the track to come above black *picon* fields and a hut (Wp.13 25M) just before the track runs out (28M) for us to come onto a narrow walking trail running behind the northern edge of the fields. A white painted cairn marks a small gully (Wp.14) cairns ahead of us marking our trail's route to climb up onto a spur of the main ridge. Across an affluent and the trail is less distinct, as we ascend from the corner of the last field (Wp.15) to cross another affluent.

Across two more affluents in this furrowed landscape and we're climbing the cairned path, the final cairn (Wp.16) appearing as a 'head & shoulders' from lower down the trail. A final climb brings us onto a broad *lomo* running south-east from the main ridge, with views to **Puerto del Carmen**. Now we start climbing in earnest. A faint track leads us up the *lomo* in a slogging ascent over the barren ground. onwards and upwards we come to a faint junction (Wp.17) where we keep right to connect with our outward route. From here it's all downhill to the windmill 'tooth', where it is down left for **Yaiza**, or onwards and down right for **Uga**.

Traditionally, the route up to the **Atalaya de Femés** is a linear one from either **Yaiza** or **Uga**, described in detail in our **Atalaya de Femés** - Linear Walk description. **Femés** is a beautiful village nestling in a fold at the top of the escarpment overlooking the **Rubicón** plain, easiest to reach by hire car but also accessible by bus. So here is our circular route up the **Atalaya**, definitely both the simplest and most interesting way of taking in the peak.

Access by car:
There's plenty of parking around **Femés** village square.

Access by bus:
N°5 **Arrecife** to **Femés** leaves the bus station at 8:15 Mon to Fri only, reaching the village at approx. 09.00. There's only two N°5 buses back to **Arrecife** from here, at 14:45 and 20.00. Check these times have not been changed! See appendices at the back of this book for timetables.

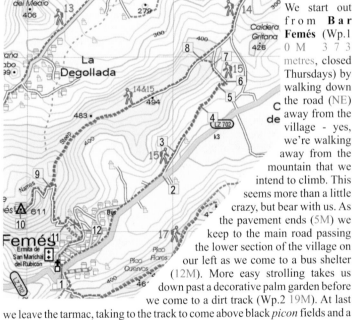

We start out from **Bar Femés** (Wp.1 0 M 373 metres, closed Thursdays) by walking down the road (NE) away from the village - yes, we're walking away from the mountain that we intend to climb. This seems more than a little crazy, but bear with us. As the pavement ends (5M) we keep to the main road passing the lower section of the village on our left as we come to a bus shelter (12M). More easy strolling takes us down past a decorative palm garden before we come to a dirt track (Wp.2 19M). At last we leave the tarmac, taking to the track to come above black *picon* fields and a hut (Wp.3 25M) just before the track runs out (28M) and we come onto a narrow walking trail running behind the northern edge of the fields.

A white painted cairn marks a small gully (Wp.4), cairns ahead of us marking our trail's route to climb up onto a spur of the main ridge. Across an affluent, the trail becomes less distinct as we ascend from the corner of the last field (Wp.5) to cross another affluent. Across another two affluents in this furrowed landscape, and we are climbing the cairned path, the final cairn

(Wp.6 44M) resembling a 'head & shoulders' from lower down the trail. A final climb brings us onto a broad *lomo* running south-east from the main ridge, with views over to **Puerto del Carmen**.

Now we start climbing (NW) in earnest. A faint track leads us up the *lomo* in a slogging ascent over barren ground. Onwards and upwards, we come to a faint junction (Wp.7). We keep straight ahead, but if returning to **Uga** or **Yaiza** swing right at the junction to connect with your outward route, the track dwindling to nothing as we cross the rock-littered open ground before coming onto the clear track of the traditional linear route running up the *lomo* (Wp.8 61M). Our steady ascent brings us onto a plateau on the wide ridge; for once the walking becomes an easy stroll as we saunter past rocky outcrops which provide sufficient moisture and shelter for plant life to thrive, in contrast to the barren landscape we have been walking through. After skirting the outcrops, and with the peak's aerials ahead, our track dwindles to a path across a narrow section of the ridge and a small descent before we face a stiff 'puff and grunt' climb. The steep climb - stairs cut in the trail would be most useful - brings us up onto a trackless plateau where cairns guide us front left over to the start of a faint track which takes us onto the **Atalaya**'s access road (Wp.9 98M).

Once on the broad dirt road navigation, which has not been at all difficult to this point, becomes simplicity itself. We head up the broad track climbing up through a zigzag to look down into a 'named' *caldera* and then straight uphill slog to the peak's trig point (Wp.10 107M) beside the buildings and aerials. Going to the far end of the buildings we find a stepped path leading down to a cave house; just the place to take off your backpack and relax. The two small rooms and plastered walls appear to predate the transmitters, and a path leads on to a second smaller cave also shaped for habitation.

Descent to **Femés**

From the trig point, **Femés** village square looks both inviting and deceptively close. Our descent is so straightforward (we just head down the access track) that no description is necessary except to say, take care. The track is eroded in places and has a loose grit/dust surface in others making for a skittery descent with the possibility of being unceremoniously dumped on your bottom; we know!

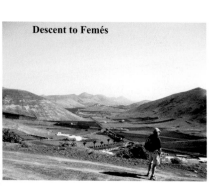
Descent to Femés

We pass our upward route (Wp.9 8M) and after a series of zig-zags we pass a track going steeply down to our right (Wp.11 23M). After the chained vehicle barrier we come onto a village dirt road (Wp.12 32M) to go right and pass the bottom of the track we saw earlier. Reaching the village houses, we come onto tarmac/concrete streets where keeping straight ahead brings us into the village square and **Bar Femés** (Wp.1 42M) with more scenically positioned refreshments available a short stroll away on the edge of the **Femés** escarpment.

Safe from the depredations of tourism is a region of barren grandeur comprising the **Higuera** and **Casita** barrancos. Fifteen years ago when we discovered this route it was little-known, though it's now become relatively popular with energetic walkers. The only development since we first walked the route consists of a basic refuge near its half way point. It might be called a refuge but it offers negligible shade, so set out well protected and with plenty of water for this adventure in the wilderness. Clear paths make for easy route finding, with the exception of finding our outward path by the goat farm.

Access by car: park in Femés.

Short Walk

Follow the route in reverse to ascend **Pico Aceituna** and return the same way. 1.5 hours, 4 kilometres, 200 metres ascents/descents.

Access by bus:

N°5 **Arrecife** to **Femés** leaves the bus station at 8:15 Mon to Fri only, reaching the village at approx. 09.00. There's only two N°5 buses back to **Arrecife** from here, at 14:45 and 20.00. Check these times have not changed! See appendices at the back of this book for timetables.

We start in the village of **Femés** outside the bar of the same name. Across the 'main' road we start out on a tarmac road (Wp.1 0M 376 metres) heading south (S) towards a ridge topped with an ugly farm. The tarmac soon gives way to dirt as we start a slogging ascent up towards the farm, passing two paths on our right before struggling up to the end of the track beside the goat farm on the ridge (Wp.2 7M) to

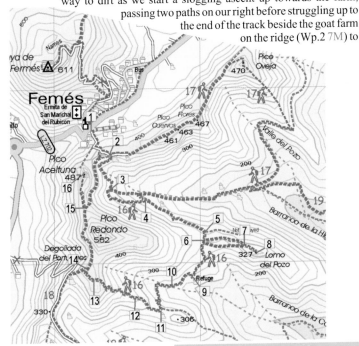

look down into the **Barranco de la Higuera**. Here the ground is churned up by the goats which can confuse the confuse-able as to where the path is. Keeping the main farm and corral on our left, we step to the edge of the ridge.

Away on our right is our return path, clearly outlined against

Walking signs and goats on top of the ridge

The start of the descent

the rock, while below us our dusty narrow path drops down into the *barranco*. It is a skittery descent on the loose, goat-churned surface, dropping past multi-hued rocks to turn below **Pico Aceituna** (and the return path) to start a zigzag descent down to a cobbled section (18M).

Now we are on an undulating easy section of path which heads towards an electricity pylon, **Puerto Calero** coming into view in the distance. We wind steadily downhill, passing Nicotiana plants struggling to survive in this barren landscape.

Passing a path to our left (Wp.3 27M) (our original route, and an option to finish in **Playa Quemada**) we start turning into and out of the affluents which feed the main *barranco* before we come under the pylon to step onto an old jeep track (30M). A path connects sections of the old track as we follow the line of the pylons; ahead we can see our trail's extension as we pass a path coming up from our left (Wp.4, our original route) before coming down to a second pylon.

From the pylon, we ignore traces heading into the *barranco* as we start heading up the main path which climbs up past a crumbling corral and crossing an affluent before a slogging ascent brings us up past great swathes of Asphodels to meet the ridge's crest at a broad saddle.

On reaching the saddle we find a wide stone-littered plain, on our left another trace/path down to **Playa Quemada** (Wp.5) while our route continues ahead as a swept path through the rock litter. An easy stroll takes us over to a junction (Wp.6 55M) where a jeep track and a path head left (E) to the small peak of **Morro de la Loma del Pozo**.

Having come this far it would be foolish to ignore the extension to the *morro* (literally, the snout or nose) so we head out on the narrow path, an easy stroll until we close with the peak where the gradient increases by the first outcrop. The jeep track comes up to join us (Wp.7) - not that you'd want to drive anything on this track - for a steep ascent up to a pair of large cairns which mark the summit (Wp.8 66M). We return to the junction (Wp.6 80M) on the jeep track.

Back on the main route, we head SW on the path, the refuge coming into sight like a mirage in this barren expanse. Our path heads down through an affluent to bring us to the refuge (Wp.9 86M), perched on the edge of the **Barranco de la Casita**.

Relaxing at the refuge

We give thanks to the authorities who have constructed a refuge in the middle of nowhere, and honour the construction with our presence for a break; if only they had put a proper roof on it to provide some meaningful shade.

Relaxing at the refuge, we can appreciate the subtle variations of the rock hues in this arid environment, as well as contemplating the task ahead of us as we sit under the looming presence of **Pico Redondo**.

From the refuge (0M) we follow the path as it winds down into a gully, after which our path unwinds along the side of the big *barranco*, crossing a couple of affluents before coming into the ravine proper to run down to cross the line of the watercourse (Wp.10). Standing on the *barranco* floor, we appreciate that the next stage is of necessity energetic. All around us the land rises up to high ridges and to **Pico Redondo**, none of it vertical but all of it muscle-sappingly steep. Looking up the ravine we can see our next objective, the high saddle to the left of **Pico Redondo**, and very high up it appears from this viewpoint.

Our broad path angles up the southern slope before swinging left for a long traverse up onto the ridge which separates us from **Barranco de los Dises**, a 'puff and grunt' ascent up through zigzags bringing us onto the ridge by an old corral (Wp.11 17M 295 metres) to look longingly back to the refuge. Now our path heads straight up the ridge, getting rougher as we come up to pass a rocky peak thick with asphodels (Wp.12 343 metres).

Ahead, our path zigzags up a steeper section of the *lomo*, yet another 'puff and grunt' ascent, taking breaks at each turn. This relentless slog up the *lomo* is brightened by the flocks of goats of all shades and sizes that we always find on this ridge. The goats are not quite pettable but give a bemused look at us strange bipeds who make such hard

... bemused goats ...

work of the rocky ground that they simply skip over.

Eventually our ascent brings us up onto the saddle between **Pico Redondo** and **Hacha Grande** (Wp.13 48M 449 metres).

From the saddle, a narrow path curves right around the peak's western slopes to bring us above a goat farm set on a saddle fifty metres below us. We come down to a path junction (Wp.14 52M) where the **Femés-Papagayo** route goes down to the farm and dirt road. Keeping right, our narrow path, and a black water pipe, curve round a steep bowl (possibly vertiginous for some) past bands of soft hued rock before a short ascent takes us over a spur into a smaller bowl. **Pico Aceituna** is ahead as we come up past deep purple rock to emerge onto the saddle between **Redondo** and **Aceituna**. (Wp.15 72M).

Here we take a diversion off the main route to climb **Pico Aceituna**. A faint path leads up the lower slopes but soon disappears amongst the rocks. We simply keep climbing straight up, picking our steps over the rocks to come onto the summit (Wp.16) beside a large stone corral which has been built in this least likely location. From the northern end of the peak we look down on **Femés**, while the views over the **Rubicón** plain to **Playa Blanca** and **Fuerteventura** are a fitting reward for this small ascent.

It is possible to scramble down the northern face of the peak - possible, but not recommended, and so we retrace our upward route back to the saddle (Wp.15). We leave the saddle on a narrow path dropping down into the **Barranco de la Higuera**, our route curving round beneath **Aceituna** before climbing up to the goat farm ridge by a second building. We take a path down the slope in front of the building to join the dirt road for a relaxed stroll down to the village centre, where a choice of refreshment opportunities should not be overlooked; **Bar Femés** is closest and least touristy but also the least picturesque.

Femés is a favourite with us. Way back in 1995, our 'Hidden Barrancos' route pioneered walking in the **Higuera** and **Casita** *barrancos*, our route now appearing in other books and our subsequent routes being the basis of the new wayposting in this previously neglected region.

Femés Ridge is one of the few Lanzarote routes where you get close to a high mountain feeling, yet we reach the mountain peak in a relatively relaxed manner on a little-known path, plus some open ground climbing. We have magnificent views from **Pico Oveja** (Sheep Peak) over the southern peaks, before descending into the valleys. You cannot get that high - and that low - on a circular route, without the inevitable uphill finish; a long slog up through the old Majo settlement in the **Barranco de la Higuera**. Quite simply, a modern classic route for experienced walkers.

Access by car:
Park in the centre of Femés near the church square.

Short Walk
To **Pico Oveja** and return (3 Walker, 1¾ hours).

Access by bus:
N°5 **Arrecife** to **Femés** leaves the bus station at 8:15 Mon to Fri only, reaching the village at approx. 09.00. There's only two N°5 buses back to **Arrecife** from here, at 14:45 and 20.00. Check these times have not changed! See appendices at the back of this book for timetables.

Heading up the track at the start

From **Bar Femés** (Wp.1 0M) we cross the main road to head up the track, tarmac soon giving way to dirt, towards the ugly goat farm sat on the ridge. The slogging ascent up between the water tanks and past a trail off to our right brings us up to the farm's modern door entrance (Wp.2 7M), where we continue along the track (E) to head over a crest to a second farm (Wp.3 12M) with noisy chained dogs.

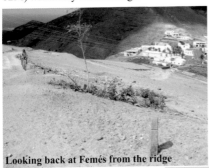
Looking back at Femés from the ridge

The track ends as we continue on the northern side of the ridge following a trail - really a mere trace of a goat trail - to maintain height as we head towards the first of the peaks. When one trace finishes we simply step onto another, a path gradually emerging as we come below the first peak (Wp.4), a rocky scramble if you want to take in the views.

Black *picon* fields dot the **Femés Valley** below us, while ahead in the distance are the **Timanfaya Fire Mountains (Montañas del Fuego)**, but no views south until the rocky ridge runs down to a 'rock free' crest where we step up from the path to marvel at the southern landscapes.

Back on the path, we maintain height until our path starts running downhill to a saddle, the surface becoming rock-littered, slowing our progress before disappearing entirely in a maze of goat traces. From the saddle, we climb up to a boulder-mounted cairn on the ridge (Wp.5 28M) for more breathtaking views into the valleys.

From the cairn, we continue along the ridge saddle past a pair of *zoco* style small corrals, a faint path emerging as the ridge rises again on our right to **Pico Oveja**. Maintaining height, we see ahead that our current trail runs down, becoming more defined as it descends to meet a trail from **Casitas de Femes** on a broad saddle.

Now it's decision time. We could continue on the improving trail across the

northern slopes of **Pico Oveja** and the ridge line before turning back into the 'hidden barrancos', all of it easy walking on defined trails (see map section); or we could head direct for the peak, a rather more adventurous option.

Being adventurous, we go uphill over open ground and goat traces, aiming for an old terrace; there are a few of these small boulder-supported terraces, but simply head for the highest one. Continuing diagonally uphill towards the line of the ridge, we cross another terrace before coming up to a low stone wall which runs up the ridge. Now we follow the wall until it gives out, from where a 'puff and grunt' ascent brings us up to **Pico Oveja** (Wp.6 55M).

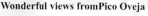
Wonderful views fromPico Oveja

Stepping around the peak itself, we move from a comparatively gentle landscape to an orogenical one. After that climb it would be a waste to immediately strike off down into the valleys, and even though there is plenty of proof that the peak is popular with goats, we find some suitable ledges at a comfortable height on the southern side, on which to be seated while taking in the views.

From our vantage point on the peak we can see the trail coming over the saddle from **Casitas de Femés**, our first objective on the descent.

This is pathless country with a picky descent, steep in places before we reach the path, so if in doubt, return by our outward route to **Femés** or backtrack to the alternative path.

We strike off from the peak (0M) along the line of the ridge (SE) carefully picking our way down to where the ridge broadens into a rock-littered *lomo*. Keeping direction (SW), we stroll down the *lomo*, surrounded by superb views, to its 'nose' (Wp.7). The steep 'nose' calls for care as we pick our way down over loose rock and boulders. Taking a break on this picky descent we can see the trail from **Casitas** coming over a saddle, still a long way ahead and down from our position.

At the base of the 'nose' we look back at the line of our descent - it looks almost sheer from below (!), before resuming a strolling descent of the rock-littered *lomo* to pass the remains of a corral (Wp.8) and finally come down to the trail (Wp.9 36M), positively a 'walking motorway' in these pathless expanses. From here you could turn left for **Casitas** and return to **Femés** on the road, an easier but less spectacular route than what we have ahead. Once on the path, we follow it right, our route feeling comfortably luxurious after the *lomo*, to start dropping (NW) into the **Valle del Pozo**.

After heading up the valley and gradually descending, we come down to cross a water runoff by an old stone wall (Wp.10 41M). Across the runoff, our trail swings left (SSE) down towards the main valley and a line of small electricity pylons.

Our faint path crosses another runoff and follows old stone walls, this section giving a wonderful sense of spaciousness as we stroll down to cross more runoffs before swinging right (SSW) into the main valley where we come alongside a jeep track, which our path joins by an electricity pylon (Wp.11 52M).

We've been descending continuously for nearly an hour, and now we face the consequences in the form of a long uphill slog along the **Barranco de la Higuera**. Setting off from the pylon we follow the jeep track beside the broad water runoff. As we climb this relentless ascent, we start to pass old corrals and stone walls before crossing the runoff (Wp.12) which now becomes a small gorge on our right. Technically, the jeep track should be an easy section of our route, but it doesn't feel like it as we labour up past pylons, corrals and stone walls before crossing an affluent (Wp.13) which brings the hideous goat farms into view high up on the ridge ahead; and before you ask the answer is, 'Yes, we *do* have to climb up there!'.

The remains of corrals and buildings litter the valley floor, some thought to be remains of Majo settlements (the eastern Canary Islands' equivalent of the western islands' Guanches), pre-dating the Spanish invasion. A second division of this agricultural settlement was based around the mouth of the *barranco* at **Playa del Pozo**. There have been some archaeological investigations made of these ruins; their Majo heritage seems well proven.

We keep slogging up the rough jeep track, passing a trail off to our left (our original route in 'The Hidden Barrancos') (Wp.14) and crossing an affluent where the track swings up to our left and we continue ahead on a clear trail.

The path junction at 94 minutes

This trail climbs steeply up to join our 'Hidden Barrancos' route at a path junction (Wp.15 94M) which provides us with a good place to take a break before tackling the final ascent up to the farms.

From the junction, our narrow trail climbs steeply (N), though this style of ascent is more pleasing than the jeep track, and is enlivened by the wonderful geological examples that we pass before finally emerging from the head of the *barranco* beside the farm (110M). After that long and energetic ascent, we stumble back down the dirt track and across the road to fall into **Bar Femés** (Wp.1 115M) for some well-earned refreshment, where we can re-live the wonders of this modern classic that we've just completed.

18 FEMÉS TO PLAYA BLANCA

The long route out of **Playa Blanca** via **Papagayo** beach and up the dirt track to the **Degollada del Portugués**, followed by path and track into **Femés**, is one of Lanzarote's classic long distance routes. As with many of the island's long linear routes, accessibility is a problem. After an initial climb out of **Femés** we skirt around **Pico Aceituna** on our 'Hidden Barrancos' route (Walk 16) in reverse, before dropping down to the **Degollada del Portugués**. From this pass, we stroll down a dirt track to emerge from the mountains onto the far south of the **Rubicón** desert plain. Our official route then wanders along the coast, with the opportunity of testing the famous beaches of this region, before heading into **Playa Blanca** on the return route of Walk 10 and Walk 8 to reach the 'old town'.

Both Noel Rochford (Landscapes) and Paddy Dillon (Cicerone) describe this route as an energetic uphill from **Playa Blanca**. Why they should choose to travel this route by the most difficult approach is a mystery to us.

Access from Playa Blanca: taxi to **Femés**.

Access by bus:
N°5 **Arrecife-Femés** leaves at 8:15 Mondays to Fridays only; you should reach **Bar Femés** at approximately 09.00. There's a regular N°60 services back from **Playa Blanca** to **Arrecife**. See appendices at the back of this book for timetables.

Fine views on the descent

Access by car: drive to **Femés**, and park by the village square and taxi back from **Playa Blanca**.

2CSK Route (see P.17) though make sure you start from **Femés** end of the route. Park the lower car as described for Walk 10 'Papagayo Beach', and reduce distance to 19 kilometres.

We start out from **Bar Femés** (Wp.1 0M); if you're walking our routes in order, you'll be a well-known regular in this little bar by now. Following Walks 16 & 17 onto the ridge, we then take Walk 16 in reverse (Wp.2 11M) to come onto the pass between **Pico Aceituna** and **Pico Redondo** (Wp.3 24M).

The path below **Pico Redondo** is a little trickier, and might cause vertigo sufferers a little trouble, before reaching the path junction (Wp.4) above the goat farm, where we follow the black water pipe down past the farm and onto the **Degollada del Portugués** (Wp.5 43M).

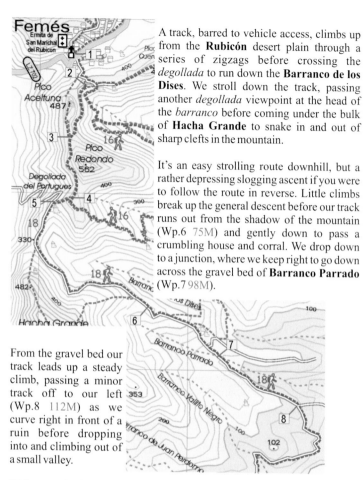

A track, barred to vehicle access, climbs up from the **Rubicón** desert plain through a series of zigzags before crossing the *degollada* to run down the **Barranco de los Dises**. We stroll down the track, passing another *degollada* viewpoint at the head of the *barranco* before coming under the bulk of **Hacha Grande** to snake in and out of sharp clefts in the mountain.

It's an easy strolling route downhill, but a rather depressing slogging ascent if you were to follow the route in reverse. Little climbs break up the general descent before our track runs out from the shadow of the mountain (Wp.6 75M) and gently down to pass a crumbling house and corral. We drop down to a junction, where we keep right to go down across the gravel bed of **Barranco Parrado** (Wp.7 98M).

From the gravel bed our track leads up a steady climb, passing a minor track off to our left (Wp.8 112M) as we curve right in front of a ruin before dropping into and climbing out of a small valley.

We're now in the tumbled lands that make up the foothills of the southern mountains, a rather depressing area where we follow the track into a valley and climb out the far side to find another similar valley ahead.

If you wonder why you've not seen any vehicles on the track, your question is answered at the notorious 'suzuki trap' (Wp.9 144M) where the water runoff effectively seals the route to all but the toughest all-wheel drive vehicles. There are still plenty of runoffs to cross before we come to the last one (Wp.10 189M) where a final climb-out brings us onto the edge of the **Rubicón** desert plain at a track junction (Wp.11 197M).

From the foot of the mountains we look out over the hazy plain to the headland bar above **Papagayo** beach and the white scars that are the eastern outskirts of **Playa Blanca**, and we have a problem. Until now, wayfinding has simply meant keeping to the main track, but now we have a plethora of tracks and trails to choose from with few identifiable landmarks to guide us. If you want the quickest way to the bar, then follow a track WSW and then forking S to come onto the main track serving the **Papagayo** parking area.

Our final objective, Playa Blanca, is in sight

Our scenic route goes SE on a track and then follow coastal paths - plenty to choose from, to either drop into beaches such as **El Pasito** (a strange glitch caused us to lose our GPS track at this point; possibly distracted by naturists, we forgot to power up after taking a break on the beach), or pass above the bays where possible.

Our scenic route is a bit longer in distance and time for us to arrive at the **Papagayo** bars (Wp.12 253M) a few minutes behind those taking the shorter dirt track alternative.

From **Papagayo** we follow Walk 10 back to the road system below the **Papagayo Arena Hotel** (1.5 km 45M). On the roads follow the blue 'Papagayo Beach' signs in reverse down to a small roundabout, and then on walkways down to the pebble beach of **Playa del Afe**; you could reach this point by staying to seaward of the hotel, and descending on paths directly onto the beach.

From the end of the beach, the coastal promenade (Walk 8) starts, guiding us into the centre of **Playa Blanca** at the 'old town' (4 kilometres +60M).

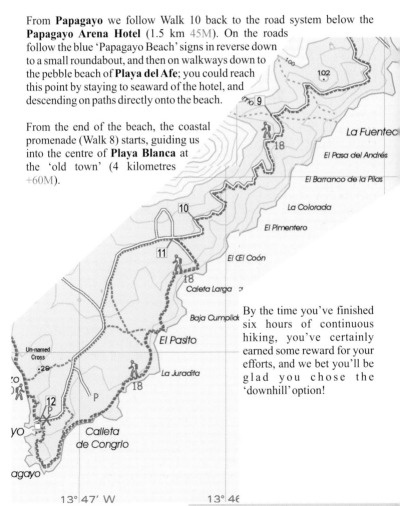

100

102

oro 9

18

La Fuentec

El Pasa del Andrés

El Barranco de la Pilas

10

La Colorada

El Pimentero

11

El Œl Coón

18

Caleta Larga

Baja Cumplida

El Pasito

Un-named Cross
·29

La Juradita

18

12
P

yo

Calleta
de Congrio

agayo

By the time you've finished six hours of continuous hiking, you've certainly earned some reward for your efforts, and we bet you'll be glad you chose the 'downhill' option!

13° 47' W

13° 46

19 FEMÉS TO PLAYA QUEMADA - THE MISSING LINK

Having pioneered the 'Hidden Barrancos' (Walk 16) route fifteen years ago, we are pleased to add the exciting circular route 'Femés Ridge' (Walk 15), and this very pleasant linear route from **Femés** to **Playa Quemada** to our repertoire. After the ascent up to the goat farm ridge, it's all downhill along the **Barranco de la Higuera** to **Playa del Pozo** then a final section on the tracks and trails of our 'Playa del Pozo' (Walk 20) route to finish in **Playa Quemada**.

There's a slight risk of vertigo in the early stages of the route (see Walk 16 'Hidden Barrancos'). We've kept our description to a minimum as once you are past the goat farm, trail finding is easy - you don't want your head in a book when you have an easy walking route through impressive scenery to enjoy.

The opening up of this easy linear route presents a myriad of opportunities to combine sections of our 16, 17 and 19 routes with other paths in the region to produce a wide variety of 'pick & mix' walking combinations.

Access by bus:
N°60 **Arrecife** to **Yaiza** then taxi to **Femés**. N°5 **Arrecife** to **Femés** leaves **Arrecife** bus station at 8:15 Mondays to Fridays only, reaching **Femés** at approximately 09:00.

Access by car:
Park either by the square in **Femés** or in **Playa Quemada** near where the road swings right by the first restaurant. In either case you will have to re-walk the route to get back to your car; so it's probably best to start in **Playa Quemada** - then you get an easy return after lunch.

It's our usual start after coffee at **Bar Femés** (Wp.1 0M) to climb up the track to the ugly goat farm from where we take the 'Hidden Barrancos' trail (Wp.2 9M) down into the head of the **Barranco de la Higuera**.

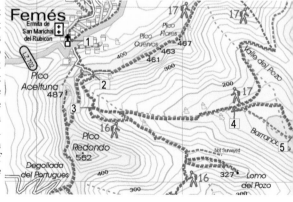

Dropping swiftly down below **Pico Aceituna**, we come to the path junction (Wp.3 16M) to go left down the *barranco* on our 'Femés Ridge' route in reverse, a much easier option than the ascent on Walk 17. An easy strolling descent takes us down past the remains of Majo (Guanche) settlements to the pylon path junction (Wp.4 39M) where our 'Femés Ridge' route comes in from the **Valle del Pozo**.

Keeping to the jeep track, we move away from the line of the water runoff in the *barranco* (E) until we meet the runoff from **Valle del Pozo** to swing right (SSW) towards **Playa del Pozo**. We come back to the **Barranco de la Higuera** runoff (Wp.5 50M) to head down the broad valley, crossing the mouth of **Barranco del Fraile** (Wp.6 63M) to come to the track climbing up the eastern wall (Wp.7). Now we're on our 'Playa del Pozo' route, leaving the track to go onto the walking trail (Wp.8).

When we come to a lower path below us on our right we have a choice of following the main path on the inland route (Wp.9) or of following the lower path across the headlands and *barrancos* (Wp.10), both routes coming together again before we come to the outskirts of the **Playa Quemada** settlement (Wp.11 95M).

Approaching Playa Quemada

Rather than follow the roads, we take the coastal path across to the sea front houses and restaurant (Wp.12 105M).

Extension to Puerto Calero (add 35 mins and 1.8km
Our finish is already on the route of Walk 2; we simply continue east on the little access road. As we climb up to the last houses, **Puerto Calero** marina comes into view. Taking the coastal path from the end of housing, we follow Walk 2 in reverse onto the promenade, as far as the marina entrance where we turn left up the road to the bus stop by the roundabout. (Bus N°61)

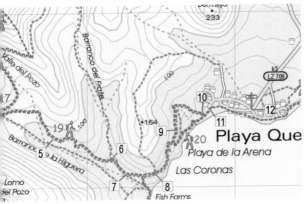

Playa Quemada is literally the end of the road, but this doesn't mean that it's the end of exploring - far from it. Sections of this coastal exploration route get quite busy in a rather bizarre fashion, as the many people who head for the **Playa de la Arena** beach clad in the most minimalist gear contrast wildly with the *parapentes* who labour up to their launch point with enormous back packs. Once away from the first section of the route you're into barren tranquility, strolling above the cliffs before dropping into the large **Barranco de la Higuera** to find a few cozzie-optional hikers enjoying the isolated beach of **Playa del Pozo**.

Extension	**Short Walk**
This route can be extended into an ascent up to **Femés**, 7km, Ascents 550 metres; see Walk 19.	To **Playa de la Arena** and return.

Access by car:
Drive through **Playa Quemada** as far as you can. At the far end of the settlement keep left to come onto a cul-de-sac on the seaward side of the houses where there is parking for 8-10 cars.

The steep zigzag ascent

From beside the parking area (Wp.1 0M), a broad trail climbs up onto the headland to a cairn (Wp.2) above the first bay. This whole region is criss-crossed by a mixture of trails which can cause confusion, so we recommend staying on the main trail.

Ahead, a clear trail zigzags up from the *barranco* behind **Playa la Arena** as we start curving into the *barranco* to a zigzag descent. Taking care on the slippery surface, we drop down to a path junction (8M) where most people go left and down to the **Playa de la Arena** beach. We continue straight on, to climb the steep zigzag ascent onto the next headland, taking it one zig or zag at a time.

Our ascent brings us up to a T-junction (16M) whose right hand branch is an alternative return route avoiding the descent and ascent through the *barranco*. Going left, we immediately hit another junction. Here the main path goes right to zigzag up the steep lomo to the *parapente* launch point, while we take the minor path straight ahead.

We are now above the cliffs as we swing into a *barranco*, and ignoring a trace path descending, we stay on the narrow path to cross the *barranco*'s water runoff.

Coming out of the *barranco*, the trace joins us and we have a choice of higher or lower paths; it is quite amazing how this region has so many tracks and paths when it has not previously featured in any guide book.

Taking the higher path, we curve round into another *barranco*, and as our path runs out we find another couple of paths running into the *barranco*. In this myriad of traces we maintain altitude by stepping up onto the higher path off to our right (Wp.3 22M); our alternative return route winds inland, avoiding the steep ascents and descents by **Playa de la Arena**. Ignoring the many traces, we come along to cross the water runoff of the side *barranco*, then emerge from the side *barranco* and immediately curve around the main *barranco* to finally emerge above the cliffs and azure sea.

Our route is very much into and out of *barrancos* interspersed with sea views, as we cross yet another small water runoff and stay on the best defined path out of this *barranco* from where our destination of **Playa del Pozo** comes into view (32M). It might look close, but there are still a few obstacles in the way. We turn into a small but precipitous *barranco* where the stone -littered path deserves careful footwork before crossing the water runoff; emerging, we have a choice of walking trail or dirt/stone track for our descent into **Barranco de la Higuera**.

The sculptor at work

Across from us on the opposite wall of the *barranco* is an enormous stone design, a maritime anchor-style design which was just being finished by the local sculptor when we were last on this route - if you look closely at the photo, you can just about make out the artist at the top right of his design. His presence gives a good impression of the size of his work.

Taking the walking trail, we descend until the path peters out and than transfer to the rubble-ised track. It looks as if we would have to go a long way up the ravine, but look for a walking trail leaving the track (Wp.4 40M). The narrow path drops us down towards the *barranco* floor, a cairn marking the last traverse before we come onto a track (Wp.5) running along the ravine floor.

The refuge at Playa del Pozo

Going left, we follow the track to the mouth of the *barranco*, where it swings right behind the boulder beach to bring us across to the refuge (Wp.6 62M) and *pozo* from which the beach takes its name. There is little, if any, shade at **Playa del Pozo** so make sure you are well protected against the sun.

Our return is a retracing of our outward route until we reach the junction at Wp.3 (46M) where we keep straight on instead of dropping into the *barranco*. Our path runs inland, and as is the way of this area, a second path parallels our route twenty metres lower down the *barranco*, gently descending slopes covered with goat traces. We are heading towards a junction of barren valleys that con-join inland of **Playa de la Arena**. At a faint junction (Wp.7) a trace goes ahead while our path turns right, its continuation is clearly seen across the valley, for us to join the second (lower) at the gravel-lined water course. Now we have a steady ascent up the grit-surfaced path, easier to ascend than descend, to come onto a faint track which runs along the *lomo*. We head back down the track towards the sea to rejoin our outward route.

PLAYA DEL POZO

It's thought that when the Normans invaded Lanzarote in 1402 under Jean de Béthencourt, the beach of **Playa del Pozo** became one of their first settlements. In the 1950s the Serra Ráfols brothers carried out archaeological investigations revealing the remains of a tower, a church, dwellings, wells, and a burial area. Other historians believe that the remains of the water channelling and well system, complete with triangular rock carvings, point to the Phoenicians as the first settlers. The *pozo* on the beach is a restoration of one of the original wells.

The most difficult thing about this walk is getting a place on the walk itself. This is the official guided walk in the **Timanfaya** and you need to book by phoning the Visitors' Centre on 928-840839, or calling in person; the centre is on the LZ67 road south of **Tinajo** and **Mancha Blanca**.

Numbers are limited to two mini buses, each carrying seven walkers and at the time of preparing this edition, the walks go on Monday, Tuesday, Thursday and Friday. Given the increasing popularity of this guided walk, it is getting even more difficult to secure one of the fourteen places available so we recommend phoning (00-34-928-840839 when dialling from outside Spain), well before you leave for Lanzarote. You'll need to reconfirm your place on the walk the day before by phone or visit.

Access by car:
On the LZ67 road from **Yaiza** to **Mancha Blanca**. Drive past the entrance to **Timanfaya National Park**, and the Visitors' Centre is the next major building on your left, 3.5 kilometres further along the road. Make sure you arrive before the 10.00 start.

2CSK Route (see P.17)

Malpais and lapilli lava

Assuming you've managed the rather difficult task of securing a place, then at 10.00 it's all aboard the two buses, followed by a long drive via **Yaiza**.

This will be either on your outward or return trip, depending on which bus you are in.

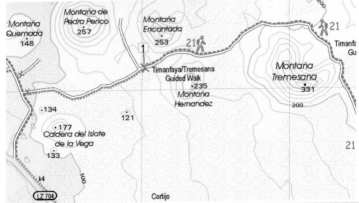

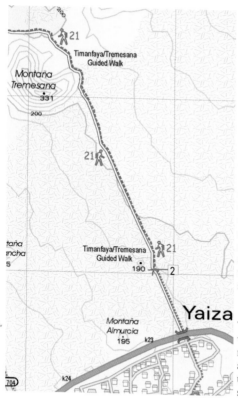

Depending on the group, you'll either have a bit of uphill or downhill during your route, but this is hardly noticeable due to the slow nature of the walking lecture tour. It's an interesting tour amongst almost virgin lava, with examples of volcanic tubes or *jameos*, including one you can stand in, and you'll learn about the different types of lava: the *lapilli*, or fine ash, the *malpais* or 'AA' scoria lava which is sharp and jagged, the *pahoehoe* type that has set in smooth swags, and lava bombs.

The guides are well versed in the facts and myths of the **Timanfaya** as we amble through the unique landscape on this strolling lecture tour.

They park the buses at each end of the manicured track (Wps. 1&2) and swap keys when they meet - wonder where they got that idea from? If they think you are capable, (basically, if all of you look like you can walk and there are no 'couch potatoes' in the group) they will do the full 'there and back' walk of six kilometres in only a little more than the one way time. For everyone interested in the historical and volcanic background of the **Timanfaya**, this is a 'Must Do' tour, though you will have to sift the fact from myth; for example, if …"a footstep takes three years to disappear …." then why is there no sign of the workers' footmarks who created this manicured track?

At the risk of exposing yourself to Lanzarote's 'lava police', you could walk the route yourself without guides. Just <u>saying</u> this is possibly a treasonable offence on Lanzarote, but the track is open to public access. At each end a padlocked chain bars vehicle access, for which the guides and farmers have keys, but it is open for walkers. If you cannot get a place on the official walk, or would be unhappy at the very pedestrian pace, simply park at one end of the access track and walk in and back; alternatively, be a two car group and park a car at each end and swap keys when you meet amongst the lava.

Once in a while we discover an absolute gem of a walking route, something not in any other guide book, and which even the authorities have missed. **Montaña Cuervo** is just such a gem, so much so that if you miss this little route you will miss much of what Lanzarote has to offer. Vulcanologists will marvel at the condition of the exploded volcanic cone, while the rest of us simply stare in awe at the truly spectacular *caldera*.

Don't try to compare this natural wonder with the sanitised **Timanfaya** bus ride or closely guided walks - nothing compares to **Montaña Cuervo**. However, judging by the access track and car park near the cone, the authorities might be planning to make this another 'loads-a-money' attraction, so best to see this natural wonder now while it's as free as the Lanzarote wind.

The mystical Montaña Cuervo

20m
20m
4 km

0

Access by car:
On the LZ56 park on the roadside just north of the **Tías/Tinajo** municipal boundary markers, or pull into the car parking area on the east of the road a few metres further north.

Short Walk
This walk is already short, but if you are only interested in the truly spectacular, then go into the *caldera* and return, remembering the path over the lava field on your return.

Extended Walk	We leave the LZ56 on a well-stabilised track (Wp.1 0M),

Extended Walk
Dirt tracks branch off our circular route enabling you to explore more of the 'lava sea' of this region. Where our track meets the cone at Wp.2, a *picon* path climbs to the lip of the crater: a gritty ascent and slidey descent, not recommended.

We leave the LZ56 on a well-stabilised track (Wp.1 0M), stepping over or round the chain barring vehicle access to head west towards the small mountain. **Montaña Cuervo** is not a big mountain, but rising up out of the lava sea, its sharp image contrasts with the fuzzy lava, lending it a mystical presence even from this distance.

An easy stroll along the cinder track takes us past a faint track, off to our right, to swing left and then right to come to the base of the cone (Wp.2 6M) where another track goes off to the right (N). We shun the steep *picon* path climbing to the lip of the crater and follow our track around the cone (NNW), a lava 'wave' cutting out the views as we pass another steep *picon* path ascending the crater shortly before coming to a surprise (Wp.3 10M); not the large car parking area on the right, but the huge gash in the side of the volcanic cone which gives access to its interior.

To descend the path beneath huge volcanic boulders into the *caldera* is to

Inside the crater ... a surreal experience

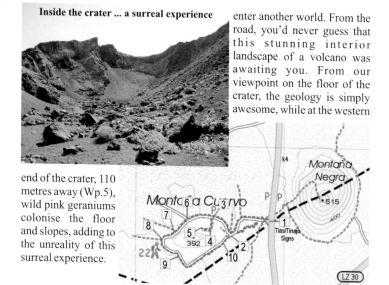

enter another world. From the road, you'd never guess that this stunning interior landscape of a volcano was awaiting you. From our viewpoint on the floor of the crater, the geology is simply awesome, while at the western end of the crater, 110 metres away (Wp.5), wild pink geraniums colonise the floor and slopes, adding to the unreality of this surreal experience.

People spend hours in this crater where time has little meaning, so when you choose to depart we'll re-start our timing at the crater entrance (Wp.3 0M) as we head west around the cone on a broad *picon* trail running between the mountain and the lava 'wave' on our right. The wave is broken by a track (Wp.6) which heads towards **Timanfaya**, the break giving us a chance to look out over this great 'lava sea'.

As we circle the extended cone, we pass another track going out into lava fields (Wp.7 8M) and admire more colonies of wild geraniums blooming in the most unforgiving landscape you could imagine, particularly numerous in one floriferous area seemingly at odds with the surroundings, which also sustains Vinagrera (Rumex lunaria), Lanzarote Firebush or Aulaga (Launaea arborescens), and Nicotiana glauca.

Our track runs gently downhill past a track heading out into the lava (Wp.8) and curves around the mountain (SSE), then passing a series of lava ledges (Wp.9) on our right, clearly indicating the thin, harder surfaced crusts above a softer core that you'll be warned not to step on if you take the **Timanfaya** guided walk. We crunch along the *picon* trail curving (WNW) towards the main bulk of the mountain rising above cinder dunes, the dunes and cinder slopes being replaced by bedrock (Wp.10) shortly before we come back to our outward route (21M) beside the path which climbs to the crater rim.

Strolling back towards the LZ56, we notice a trail marked by an arrow of stones (24M), a junction we missed on our way outward. We turn off the track onto the path which then wanders through the broken crust of the lava field giving a real, up close and personal view of lava ledges and collapsed crust, before coming back to our outward track to stroll back to the parking area. Arriving back at our car, we can only marvel at this 'gem' of an easy walking route, almost literally in the middle of nowhere.

Sometimes we set out seeking a particular objective - then fate conspires to give us something unexpected that is better. So it was, when we were looking to climb **Montaña Negra** across the LZ-56 from **Montaña Cuervo**. Every time we've been there, it's been too windy and anyway, you can clearly see the trail ascending the cone so all you need is a calm day on which to find your own way. Windy again, so we continued up the road to park south of **Caldera Santa Catalina** thinking the crushed lava track might be extended to a walk across to **Montaña Los Rodeos**; it doesn't and even if it did, the going is so rough on the broken lava as to turn it into an endurance test.

So we ended up in the large parking area at the top of the LZ-56 a bit dispirited saying "well, we might as well check out the track to **Montaña Los Rodeos**" and you'll be very glad we did. The result is a route of such comforting simplicity with good conditions underfoot that it could be regarded as a stroll suitable for all the family. Simple yet interesting, as while we get right up close to the pristine lava fields, literally 'nose to nose', we do so on an easy walking surface. We didn't climb to the peak - that wind again - but if it's calm you have the option of a hundred metre ascent/descent on a rough jeep track to take in the stunning views from the summit.

Access by car:
Park in the large parking area on the west of the LZ-56 at km0.4. Note that this is out in the country, so don't leave anything in your car while you are walking.

At the top of the parking area a tarmac lane heads NW accessing the farmed plots as it heads out to meet the LZ-67 just south of our access to Walk 39.

Starting out

We start at the junction where a dirt track heads SW off the lane (Wp.1 0M) to walk down the dirt track with **Montaña Cortijo** rising on our right in contrast to the lava plain on our left as we pass a cave/hut cut into the base of the small mountain (Wp.2 6M).

As dirt tracks go this is an immaculate top of the range example whose firm even surface makes for easy walking taking us to a junction (Wp.3 13M) where a minor track services a cultivated *picon* plot set below **Montañas Rostros** and **Cortijo**. We stay on the main track which now swings towards the south taking us directly towards **Los Rodeos**. Steadily, **Los Rodeos** dominates our view ahead until it is looming above us when we come to a T-junction (Wp.4 23M) directly facing the peak.

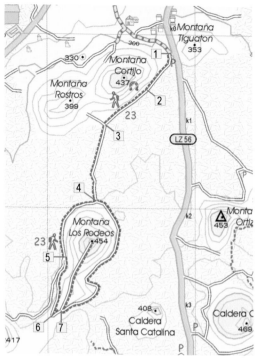

You could go either left (clockwise) or right (anticlockwise) around **Los Rodeos** but our choice is to take the right option for the views it opens up later on. As our track curves from west to south we are strolling between the mountain's slopes and a pristine area of impenetrable lava to come to an inverted Y-junction (Wp.5 32M) where one track goes front right following the edge of the Rodeos islote before cutting across the lava sea to bisect the peaks of **Caldera de la Rilla** and **Montaña del Señalo**. Our route is straight ahead, front left, on the main track as it starts ascending the *islote*. It is the first real uphill of our route, our effort immediately compensated for by the increasing views as we come onto the top of the islote (Wp.6 42M).

So far our views have been limited - this being a flat route - to looking up at the peaks and out over the western lava as we climb onto the *islote*. Now we have the eastern views. Should you think these are more of the same, lava fields dotted with volcanic cones, then look down below. Along the eastern side of the **Los Rodeos** *islote* is a green lava river, frozen where it set but its rippled surface giving the appearance of movement - it is for this view that we went right at the T-junction.

Our track continues running down the eastern side of the *islote* where eighty metres on we come to the rough jeep track (Wp.7 44M) that ascends 'straight up' to the summit of **Los Rodeos**; an ascent of just over a hundred metres giving us an energetic option to extend our route so long as the wind is not blowing. A gentle descent brings us down to the level of the lava while our track snakes around the base of the *islote* to bring us back to the T-junction (Wp.4 54M). Here we turn right to stroll back along the smooth track to the parking area (Wp.1 77M).

24 A PATH BETWEEN TWO SEAS - THE TIMANFAYA COASTAL PATH

Our third **Timanfaya** route has a surreal nature all of its own for most of the route, as we walk along a coastal path between the Atlantic Ocean on our right and the 'Lava Sea' on our left. It is long and linear so best suited to our 2CSK approach (see P.17).

We start at the achingly lovely **Playa Madera**, and twelve kilometres later emerge from the lava sea below a beautiful villa set on a hill in the middle of nowhere. Good walking footwear is essential for this rocky lava trail if you are to avoid bruising the soles of your feet. Note that access has to be by car.

| 3 | 4½ H | 13 km | | 100m ⇕ 100m | ⇔ | 0 |

Short Walk
See El Golfo route, P.149.

Access by car:

From **Tinajo** take the minor road towards **Tenesar** coastal settlement. When the road turns sharp right, continue straight ahead on a wide, but corrugated, dirt road. Ignore all side turnings, and as the surface changes to picon look for somewhere to park; note this is six kilometres of bumpy dirt road from when you leave the luxurious tarmac. On no account try to drive down to the beach area at **Playa Madera**.

From **Yaiza** take the LZ704 road to **El Golfo**. The easiest way to identify the dirt road that you need, is to drive to the junction before **El Golfo**, signed left to 'La Hoya', turn around and the dirt road is the first one on the left as you head back towards **Yaiza**.

Turn onto the dirt road and pass two chained tracks right (the first is for the **Timanfaya** guided walk) and one left and then start looking for a parking place off the track before reaching the villa set on the slopes of **Montaña Quemada**.

From your parking place, walk down the track onto **Playa Madera** (Wp.1 0M), a wonderfully isolated black beach with the Atlantic waves crashing onto the edge of the 'Lava Sea', and climb up the path onto the lava sea.

This is a wonderful setting, with the ocean crashing against the lava and small lava points on our right, while on our left the 'lava sea' rolls away to the distant **Timanfaya** fire mountains. Amongst the lava sea are points of higher ground around which the slow moving lava flowed, known locally as *islotes*; these green islands harbour local flora

Playa Madera

which stand out in sharp contrast against the barren lava. That's about as poetic as it gets, because while the setting is dramatic, with the ocean battling the lava sea, it is very much all the same. Here, they have lava in abundance forming a massive jagged plain, and the only way across this impenetrable expanse is on the coastal path.

So it's onward, one step after another along the rocky path, stopping occasionally to take in the views, which all seem remarkably like the views you stopped for earlier. It is a strange combination of beauty and monotony; we can walk for what seems like ages and then look around to have the rather disconcerting feeling that we haven't moved since the last stop, the immediate landscape being ocean and jagged lava sea. This weird impression of not making any progress can be somewhat disturbing, but keep going.

We have 9.5 kilometres of this beautiful but monotonous landscape, before **Montaña Halcones** rises out of the jagged sea on our left, indicating that we will soon be leaving the sea. Our path finally turns away from the ocean and winds along (SSE) to meet a dirt track.

Now the landscape starts to change as the lava sea gives way to fig trees in *zocos* and occasional cultivated plots as our route heads towards **Montaña Quemada** (SE), climbing gently to bring us up to a vehicle barrier (Wp.2 258M). Even the isolated farming plots seem like the height of civilisation after all that jagged lava, as we walk up to pass beneath a luxury villa (Wp.3 264M) set on the slopes of **Montaña Quemada** above our track. Having climbed up the slope of the mountain, the track now runs down to a junction of tracks (Wp.4 270M) marked by concrete gate posts with a small commemorative shrine set in them.

Where you go from the junction depends on where you choose to finish. 2CSK walkers (see P.17) should find the second car somewhere along the onward track (SE). If you plan to finish in **Yaiza**, then take this onward track to meet the LZ704 tarmac road, and turn left for 4.5 kilometres of road walking to the big roundabout, now taking the old main road signed for **Yaiza**, for another kilometre to find the first refreshments opposite the football pitch and showground on the town's outskirts.

If you're seeking the closest civilisation or refreshment, go right at the junction. This track undulates along past farmsteads (W) before swinging left (S) to meet the LZ704. Turn right and in under a kilometre you are in **El Golfo** with a choice of tourist style *tipicos* to choose from; you should also find a taxi or two here, if not, ask in a bar.

La Geria's unique landscape is one of Lanzarote's most photographed features. At close quarters the 'grape pits' don't look that impressive, but add a bit of altitude and how that perspective changes into an amazing landscape.

Originally a linear walk from **Uga** to **Puerto del Carmen**, our circular option over **Montaña Tinasoria** is now Walk 25A; there's also the option of ascending **Montaña de Guardilama** (not on windy days though) on both routes. Now you can choose the option that suits you; either bus to **Yaiza** and do the linear walk to **Puerto del Carmen** (3 Walker), or follow the main walk to the pass and then climb **Tinasoria** as you curve back towards your outward route (3 Walker); to both of these you can add in the straight forward but tough ascent of **Guardilama** for its awesome views (5 Walker). No refreshments en-route, but there are bars in **Uga** and **Bar/Rest Gregorio** near our start. Walk 26 Uga - La Geria Circular offers a further option to explore this area; for this option, follow this walk description to Wp.8 then follow the description from page 106.

The first part of our route is on the wayposted PR LZ40.1 until waypoint 7 where we turn south for the coast while the PR LZ40.1 continues ahead to **La Asomada**; see Walk 25B Alt Finish which follows the PR LZ40.1 into Asomada.

*Timings in the walk are given for the linear route direct to **Puerto del Carmen**. For the ascent of **Guardilama** add 1 hour, 2.5km and 200 metres of ascents/descents.

Access by bus:
The Nº60 calls at **Yaiza** and **Uga**. See appendices for timetables.

We start from the bus stop by **Uga** church (Wp.1 0M) to walk (SE) down to the end of **Calle Jorge Rodriguez**. Going straight ahead, past cul-de-sacs left and right, we come up to a junction (Wp.2) where we go left on **Calle Los Arenales**, a narrow road heading NE above a new, but unused park. After a house on our right, we take a dirt road to the right which climbs steeply up to the **Teguise** road; alongside the track are our first examples of La Geria 'grape pits'. On the narrow main road, we head away from **Uga** (NW) to take the first dirt road off to the right (Wp.3 17M).

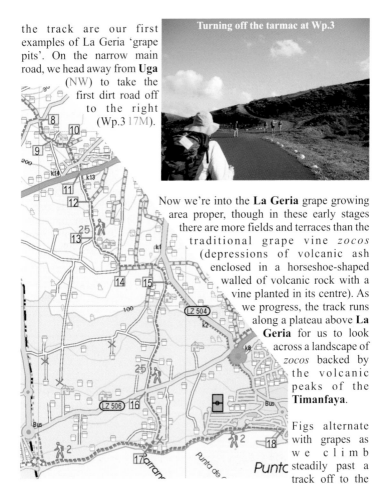

Turning off the tarmac at Wp.3

Now we're into the **La Geria** grape growing area proper, though in these early stages there are more fields and terraces than the traditional grape vine *zocos* (depressions of volcanic ash enclosed in a horseshoe-shaped walled of volcanic rock with a vine planted in its centre). As we progress, the track runs along a plateau above **La Geria** for us to look across a landscape of *zocos* backed by the volcanic peaks of the **Timanfaya**.

Figs alternate with grapes as we climb steadily past a track off to the right, the **La Geria** landscape expanding into thousands of horseshoe-shaped depressions covering the whole region. Away on our left is one of the large *bodegas* as we continue uphill past the *bodega* access track (Wp.4) towards the pass. A steady, almost slogging, ascent brings us up onto the pass (Wp.5 57M) from where we can take a break for the views over the unique **La Geria** landscape. Now, if you think these views are impressive, think what another 100 or 200 metres altitude would do.

Guardilama Option

If you are feeling fit and it's a calm day, then how about climbing **Guardilama** for the unforgettable views from its summit? Only attempt this on the calmest days as the wind sheer makes this route potentially dangerous. Not recommended for vertigo sufferers.

We go over the pass and in a few metres take a track to the left (Wp.6/Wp.8 21A) to walk up past grapes enclosed by stone walls. After the last of the stone walls the track continues straight up the mountain. This truly is a 'puff and grunt' ascent, taking frequent breaks to get our breath back. The track peters out half way up, after which we follow a faint trail straight up over the open

La Geria and Montaña Guardilama

ground; another 50 metres of ascent and a few more stops for breath sees us reach the summit (Wp.9 25A). The views are simply awesome. **Guardilama** is Lanzarote's most 'pointy' accessible peak. The **La Geria** plain lies some 300 metres below us, and the views over the volcanic cones of the **Timanfaya** are unforgettable.

Stay as long as your vertigo will allow to enjoy the island's most spectacular views. Take care on the steep descent, watching every step you make; it is all too easy to be distracted by the views and lose your footing on the steep ground.

Onward to Puerto del Carmen

From the pass we follow the dirt road down into the more familiar Lanzarote landscape, a steady descent bringing us down to a T-junction (Wp.7), **Camino del Mesón** track continuing ahead as we turn right to head downhill past a clutch of houses. We stay on the main lane, passing a nice house and track on our left, from where the lane is tarmacked, as we head down to cross the **Asomada** road (Wp.8 77M). Straight over the 'main' road, and we're back on a narrow lane to come down past **Villa Vistas** to a crossroads of tracks (Wp.9). Continuing on the tarmac lane we come down to a junction (Wp.10). Going right (S) we stroll down to the end of **Camino Los Olivos** to go left on a narrow lane, then right onto a track to carefully cross the fast and busy LZ2 main road (Wp.11).

We're back on a dusty track running (SSE) down through the general wasteland that lies between mountains and sea, a wasteland dotted with 'exclusively desirable villa residences' in estate agent speak. At the end of **Camino La Caldarina** (Wp.12 97M) we take the track to the right (S), keeping left at the next junction (Wp.13) to pass **Finca Lomos Altos** before reaching a T-junction; here we go right to come onto the end of a tarmac lane (Wp.14) at another T-junction. Going left (E) passing a lane off to the left then one to the right, we come to a lane off left to the main road. Keeping to our tarmac lane, we come to a second lane (Wp.15 120M) linking us to the **Puerto del Carmen** road.

If at this stage you are growing tired of the bungalow-dotted wasteland you could take to the main road for an easy tarmac stroll down to the *circumvalacion* roundabout, followed by pavements down into the resort.

Those of us choosing to stick with the grit head down (S) **Camino Barranco de Quiquere** past the multi-tiered garden of **Casa la Helice** for an easy stroll down past the grandly named little track of **Camino las Casanas** before coming onto the **Puerto Calero** road (Wp.16 138M). Straight over the road, we continue on the track down to the mouth of the *barranco* where we meet the route of Walk 2 (Wp.17) From here we follow the coastal path (W) back to the 'old town' of **Puerto del Carmen** (Wp.18 172M).

Walk 25 is our original route through **La Geria**, perfect if you wish to bus out from **Puerto del Carmen** to **Uga** and then walk back to the resort. Now, for walkers who wish to experience **La Geria** as the focal point of their walking route, we present our original alternative as a walking route in its own right where 90% of the walking is amongst the famous '*zocos*'.

The first part of our route is on the wayposted PR LZ40.1 until waypoint 7 where we turn uphill for **Tinasoria** while the PR LZ40.1 continues ahead to **La Asomada**; see leaflet 'PR LZ40 Red de Senderos La Geria' available from Tourist Information Offices. Also see our Alternative Finish on page 104.

Uga church at Wp.1

Our starting point is from the bus stop by the church in the centre of **Uga** (Wp.1 0M); where we usually start with coffees (café con leche) at the bar facing the church, from where we walk (SE) down to the end of **Calle Jorge Rodriguez**.

Going straight ahead, past cul-de-sacs left and right, we come up to a junction (Wp.2) that's more like a tarmac village square, where we go left on **Calle Los Arenales**, a narrow road heading NE above a new but unused park. After a house on our right, we take a dirt road to the right (Wp.3) which climbs steeply up to the **Teguise** road; alongside the track are our first examples of **La Geria** 'grape pits'. On the narrow main road we head away from **Uga** (NW) to take the first dirt road off to the right (Wp.4 17M).

Into La Geria proper

Now we are into the **La Geria** grape growing area proper, though in these early stages there are more fields and terraces growing onions than the traditional grape vine *zocos* (depressions of volcanic ash enclosed in a horseshoe-shaped walled of volcanic rock with a vine planted in its centre).

At first it's easy strolling as our track runs along a plateau above **La Geria**, passing a chained track to our right (Wp.5), for us to look across a landscape of *zocos* backed by the volcanic peaks of **Timanfaya**. Figs alternate with grapes as we climb steadily past a track off to the right (Wp.6), the **La Geria** landscape expanding into thousands of horseshoe-shaped depressions covering the whole region. Away on our left is one of the large *bodegas* as we continue uphill past the *bodega* access track (Wp.15) towards the pass. A steady, almost slogging, ascent brings us up onto the pass, from where we can take a break for the views over this unique landscape - if you think these views are impressive, think what another 100 or 200 metres altitude would do. Over the pass we are walking past a fenced field on our left as we come to the **Tinasoria** track on our right (Wp.7 55M).

Guardilama Option
See the Guardilama Option included in Walk 25 description. The waypoints 8; turn off the main track & 9; peak of **Guardilama**, are included in Walk 25A's waypoint file.

Climbing Tinasoria

The water cisterns

With the main track behind us we walk gently uphill, passing a track off to our front left (Wp.10) as we head towards a relatively modern, brick-built, but abandoned farm behind which is the rising, sweeping crescent of **Tinasoria**'s crater rim. Reaching the farm (Wp.11 65M), a handy place for a break before the final

Views over the *zocos*

ascent, we notice a collection of linked water cisterns, unusual in both their size and number given that the only ground above this altitude is the **Tinasoria** rim. Beyond the farm our track dwindles, becomes rougher, splits and rejoins, before finally coming down to trail width as our curving ascent takes us towards the peak.

During the start of this climb we lose the views as our trail is just below the rim but as we get higher we start to get views over the south-west landscape. Our trail runs out at the cairn marking the peak of **Tinasoria** (Wp.12). It's tempting to stop at the cairn for the views but if we continue a little further

along the broad crater rim we come to a rough seat thoughtfully constructed from rock slabs, just the place to take a break while taking in the magnificent views.

To return to **Uga** we could simply turn round and reverse our outward route, or, as we chose, we could continue following the rim around the crater which gives a higher altitude perspective of **La Geria** than being on the main track. It is open ground walking as the rim reduces to become a broad meadow carpeted with wild flowers more reminiscent of the **Haria** valley than the dry landscape of **La Geria**.

On the descent

The gently sloping meadow brings us down alongside the *zocos* in the *caldera* on our right, and passing a notable hole on our right, before finishing at the limit of the grape *zocos*; *caldera* on our right and the top slopes of **La Geria** on our left and ahead.

We have two choices of reaching the main track:-

Option 1: we can go over to the edge of the *zocos* in the *caldera* (Wp.13) to pick our way between the *zocos* to come onto the dirt track, then turn left to walk down out of the *caldera* before joining the main track (Wp.15).

Option 2: continue to the end of the meadow (Wp.14) where we come to the edge of the *zocos* climbing up from **La Geria** where we find a narrow trail heading (NE) between the grape pits before finishing with a *picon* scree descent down to the level of the *caldera* track, from where we walk out to join the main track (Wp.15).

Both options involve walking across intensively farmed land and while we have not had any access problems you would not want to bring large groups of walkers across this ground at the risk of upsetting the farmers.

Back on the main track we have an easy relaxed stroll back down the track, quite a contrast to the earlier ascent, with just the steeper sections requiring care not to slip on the dusty/gritty surface. Returning to **Uga**, we have a choice of bars for refreshment while contemplating our next adventure, waiting for the bus, or just chilling out.

25B LA GERIA - ALTERNATIVE FINISH IN PUERTO DEL CARMEN

At Wp.7 (0M) instead of heading downhill we go left following the 'official' PRLZ-40 along **Camino del Meson** for us to pass a dirt track on our right before the dirt track becomes tarmacked (Wp.8 8M) to continue ahead as a *camino rural* lane. We have an easy stroll along the lane before arriving at a wayposted crossroads on the LZ-502 in **La Asomada** (Wp.9 17M). Following the 'Vega de Tegoyo 1.5km' arm of the waypost, we turn left to head up the LZ-502 to the next junction marked by Supermercado Hernandez where we turn right off the main road (Wp.10 20M).

Now we simply follow the narrow road passing one street on our left, then one on our right before coming to a second street on our right, **El Cao 1**, as we get views across a valley to **Vegas de Tegoyo** and **Conil**. At the end of the houses (Nºs 28 & 28C, Wp.11 28M) we go right downhill, the tarmac becoming a dirt track as we descend to the valley floor for an easy stroll across to a wayposted cross roads at **Tegoyo** (Wp.12 36M).

Straight over the crossroads, we follow the lane across another crossroads and through housing and two cul-de-sacs on our left, as it steadily climbs to swing right in front of the highest house. Now the lane becomes a dirt track, bringing us to a T-junction (Wp.13 42M), where we take the left fork to start ascending a small ridge.

On our right, the ridge is topped by a large house, our dirt track topping the ridge and running along past the house's entrance (Wp.14 44M); on walking down its entrance drive, we discover it to be **Casa Elephante Blanco** (White Elephant), as if the owner expected the tarmac to extend this far.

With the ridge behind us, we have easy strolling along the dirt track where we ignore two tracks off to our left, the second (Wp.15 50M) opposite a house constructed from lava blocks, followed by a track off to our right. There's little of note to say of the bleak *malpais* alongside our route, except that it's easy strolling as our track runs gently downhill, passing a track to our left and then another to our right, before the dirt track joins a tarmac lane (Wp.16 56M). Now it's downhill to the LZ-501 (Wp.17 58M), just above the roundabout below the end of the LZ-2 motorway.

Taking care on the roads, we pass under the motorway to cross the second roundabout and follow the road up to the western entrance to **Tías** where we find two roads off to our right (Wp.18 62M). We take the first which angles sharp right, signed 'Camino Hoya Limpia', then runs south towards the coast. Passing a dirt road on our right, **Camino del Hondo** and then a dirt track on our left, we come to a junction (Wp.19 67M) where we leave the tarmac to follow the **Camino las Quinzuelas** dirt road - if you'd prefer an easy stroll finish, then stay on the tarmac *camino rural* which heads south-west down to meet the LZ-504, just above the large roundabout at the western end of **Puerto del Carmen**. The **Camino las Quinzuelas** runs steadily downhill (S) towards **Puerto del Carmen**, simply requiring us to stay on the main dirt track ignoring tracks to left and right until shortly after house number one we come to a junction (Wp.20 86M) where the **Camino del Puerto** goes right (W). To finish at the western end of **Puerto del Carmen** we take the **Camino del Puerto**, simply ignoring side tracks until it meets up with the *camino rural* we left at Wp.19 to emerge onto the LZ-504 above the western roundabout. Then it's an easy stroll down the road to the 'Old Town' area of the resort.

To finish in the centre of **Puerto del Carmen** we continue ahead, passing a dirt track on our left, to come down to the LZ-505 main road. We could follow the LZ-505 down into the resort or cross the main road, taking care of course, to take the minor road which accesses the hospital which then swings right to pass under the LZ-40.

We come onto the recent but little-used 'inner bypass' where we go straight across the dual carriageway onto **Calle Anzuelo** which we follow downhill to emerge on the promenade in the centre of the resort, just west of the tourist information office.

Not everyone desires a long linear walking route that finishes in Lanzarote's main resort. More than a few walkers using hire cars for their exploration ask us for circular routes, preferably with safe car parking and good refreshments. If this is you, then here's your route as we take the classic **La Geria** and convert it into a circular, based on the laid-back town of **Uga**. Our additions include one kilometre of road walking but the majority is on tracks we've not previously covered, nor are they in any other guidebook we've seen.

| 4 | 2½ H * | 11 km | 490m / 490m | ↻ | 3* |

*at start and end

Access by car:
From the LZ-2 exit at the **Uga/Femés** roundabout onto the LZ-30 then take the first street left, to park at the edge of the town - or continue into **Uga** for onstreet parking near the church.

Access by bus: Bus Nº60 between **Arrecife** and **Playa Blanca** leaves from both destinations on the hour and calls at **Uga** church, Mon-Fri with a reduced service on Sat/Sun/fiestas.

We follow the classic **La Geria** route of Walk 25 until it crosses the **La Asomada** road at (Wp.8 77M) where instead of crossing the road, we turn right to walk down the road towards the roundabout on the LZ-2. We pass two lanes on our right until, just before the roundabout (Wp.9 87M), we come to a dirt track on our right which has been 'rocked off' to prevent vehicle access.

.. expanded views ..

Leaving the tarmac we step through the boulders to follow the dirt track (W) to a junction with a more substantial dirt track (Wp.10 91M) which runs out to the LZ-2 on our left. Going right, we follow the track gently uphill to an isolated house, **Casa Cañada** (Wp.11 98M), passing it on our left to continue uphill along the track.

We pass a track on our left, which accesses a cultivated plot alongside the LZ-2, before arriving at a crossroads of tracks (Wp.12 107M). We're overlooking **Caballo Lanzarote** (SW) with views south to **Playa Quemada** and **Puerto Calero**, the sixty metres we've ascended since Wp.9 already providing us with expanded views across the southern coastal plain. From the crossroads we go right (N) for the steady ascent up the track under the shadow of **Montaña Tinasoria**. It's a steady hundred metre ascent, never steep enough to be called serious but uphill all the way for the next kilometre; if you'd like an easier return, then the track straight across the junction (W) runs across above **Caballo Lanzarote** to join the LZ-30 with only thirty metres of ascents; however, we've not walked that route.

Pointing our noses north, we head up the track across the sloping plain below **Tinasoria** to pass under the high tension power lines with their red and white poles (Wp.13 109M). **Tinasoria** looms large above us as we gradually ascend to the ridge line to find ourselves overlooking the edge of the *zocos* area (Wp.14 122M). The *zocos* in this section are of relatively recent construction, their neat appearance a contrast with the older *zocos* on the earlier section of our route; as a viewpoint over **La Geria** this is one of the best. With the ascent behind us, we follow the track along the southern side of the ridge formed by **Montaña Norte** to a goat farm on the north of the track where we get more northern views (Wp.15 130M). From here it's steadily downhill passing a faint track off to our left bisecting **Montañas Majada** and **Mojón**, followed by a strange concrete structure (a water chute?) on our left (Wp.16 136M) before our track becomes a street, lined by houses on its southern side, which takes us down to the LZ-30 at the entrance to **Casa El Morro** (Wp.17 142M).

The water chute

Carefully across the main road we walk down the street (our car access) to meet our outward route at the open area crossroads where continuing straight on brings us to our starting point beside the church square and a choice of bar/restaurants for refreshment (148M).

It's well worth strolling through this historic town, first established as a settlement by the island's original inhabitants, the *Mojos*. Cobbled streets lead between white buildings, many of which have a long and interesting history. You can visit the rather austere **Palacio Spinola** palace (open daily 10.00-17.00 in summer, until 09.00-15.00 in winter, entry fee payable) in **Plaza de la Constitución**. There are several churches, monasteries and museums worth a visit, including the prominent parish church, (16th century, with numerous later embellishments) **Iglesia de Nuestra Señora de Guadalupe**, and the old **Teatrillo Municipal de Teguise** which first opened its doors in 1825. Many of the old buildings have changed use over the years; ex-convents and erstwhile homes of the rich and influential now serve as art galleries, museums, shops and bar/restaurants while retaining original façades. At its busiest on Sunday mornings, **Teguise** street market is a magnet for both residents and visitors.

Overlooking the town on top of the peak of **Guanapay** (446 metres) perches the island's oldest castle, the 16th century **Castillo de Santa Bárbara**, rescued from dilapidation to house the **Museo del Emigrante Canario** which specialises in artefacts marking the history of migration by Lanzarote's inhabitants in their attempts to find fortune overseas. Enjoy panoramic views from the peak, or take a look inside (€3 adults, Sunday to Friday).

N.B. We have not included GPS information for this walk, as satellite coverage in the narrow streets is unreliable.

Access by car:
Parking in the **Plaza Spinola** and along the main road.

Access by bus:
In addition to the Sunday market day specials (Nºs 11, 12&13), Nºs 7, 9&10 all go via **Teguise**.

We suggest beginning this relaxed stroll with refreshments in one of the town's bars. If you arrive early, call in **Sejas Bar/Café** in **Plaza Doctor Alfonso Spínola** (06.00 until 20.00), which backs onto the old **Convento de San Francisco** (1534), no longer a convent, now housing Lanzarote's collection of religious art in the **Museo de Arte Sacro**. Leaving the bar, we turn right to walk through the *plaza,* named after the Teguise-born Doctor Spinola (1845-1905) who practiced in Lanzarote and Uruguay, where he was important in controlling a smallpox outbreak. Turning right at the north-east corner brings us onto **Calle Marqués de Herrera**, passing the **Casa del Marqués** on our left, and continuing on the few steps past the narrow street on our left to see the **Teatrillo Municipal de Teguise** which has given service as a church, hospital and children's hospice before becoming a theatre in 1825.

Doubling back, we take the narrow street which runs north on **Calle Espiritu Santu** to the great open space known as **Parque La Mareta**, although there's little evidence of greenery in this large public area. If you are fortunate enough

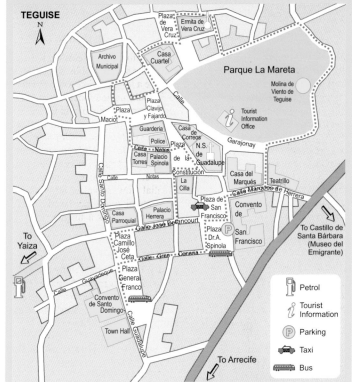

TEGUISE
N

Plaza de Vera Cruz
Ermita de Vera Cruz
Casa Cuartel
Archivo Municipal

Parque La Mareta

Molina de Viento de Teguise

Calle

Plaza Clavijo y Fajardo

Plaza Maciot

Tourist Information Office

Guardería
Police
Casa de Correos
Garajonay

Calle - Notas
Casa Torres
Palacio Spinola
Plaza de la
N.S. de Guadalupe

Calle Santo Domingo
Calle
Notas

Constitución

Casa del Marqués
Teatrillo

La Cilla

Calle Marqués de Herrera

Plaza de San Francisco

Convento de

Casa Parroquial
Palacio Herrera

Calle José Betancourt

P

Plaza Dr. A. Spinola
San Francisco

To Castillo de Santa Bárbara (Museo del Emigrante)

Plaza Camillo José Ceta

Calle Gran Canaria

To Yaiza

Plaza General Franco

Calle
Guayadeque

Convento de Santo Domingo

Calle Guadalupe

Town Hall

To Arrecife

🅿 Petrol

ℹ Tourist Information

Ⓟ Parking

🚕 Taxi

🚌 Bus

to be on the island on June 1, this square is transformed by colourful 'carpets' drawn with coloured salts.

Following its edge counter-clockwise brings us to a well preserved (except for some graffiti) windmill **Molino de Viento de Teguise**, the last remaining of twelve in this area which were used to grind cereal grains.

Parque La Mareta

El Molino de Viento de Teguise

We continue our circumnavigation of the *parque*, turning off north on the **Calle Princesa Ico** and into **Plaza de Vera Cruz** dominated by the **Ermita de Vera Cruz** with its magnificently huge doors. Leaving the *plaza* by its south-west corner, we walk to the next junction of streets where we go left (S), passing **Casa Cuartel** on our left, a former billet for

Casa Cuartel

soldiers, easily recognised by its old wooden balcony - rare on a largely treeless island.

Continuing ahead and taking a short dogleg right and left brings us into **Plaza de Clavijo y Fajardo**, where we turn right on a narrow street, at the end of which the **Archivo Municipal** faces us.

Turning left and immediately left again brings us into **Plaza Maciot**, which we walk through to leave by the narrow street in its south-east corner, then taking the next left with **Casa Torres** forming the corner, next door to the seventeenth century **Palacio Spínola** which became a museum in 1984, its walls on this side in the **Calle Notas** looking rather unstable, despite its reputation as the town's most important piee of architecture.. We step out into the main cobbled square of **Plaza de la Constitución**, the main façade and entrance to **Palacio Spínola** on its western side, and with the **Iglesia de Nuestra Señora de Guadalupe** on the opposite side, an imposing building standing out from the surrounding austere and simple architectural styles; on its north side is a building that once served as the post office, still known as **Casa de Correos** but now used by the Univerity of Las Palmas de Gran Canaria as a School of Medicine. By the south side of the church, the narrow lane **Calle Zonzamas** leads into the **Parque La Mareta**.

Cilla de Diezmos y Primicias

Also look for the seventeenth century **Caja Canarias**, on the southern edge of the square, one of the most attractive banks you are likely to see, housed in the **Cilla de Diezmos y Primicias** building once used to store grain paid as tithes - not too much of a change of use, then.

We leave the *plaza* by the street at its south-west corner, **Calle Leon y Castillo**, taking the second right onto **Calle José Betancort**, bringing us past the **Palacio Herrera** on our right - turn right around the building's corner to see its impressive wall plaque before retracing our steps back onto **Calle José Betancort** and continue in a westerly direction, passing the **Casa Paroquial** on our right. Turning left at the end of the street where it meets **Calle Guadalupe** at **Plaza Camillo José Cela** takes us past a small public garden and bus stop, opposite the **Convento de Santo Domingo** (1698), one of the town's largest buildings, and an important centre for local government offices and cultural activities in this region. It also houses the **Centro de Arte Santo Domingo** (open Mon-Fri 10.00 - 15.00, Sun 10.00-14.00). To return to our start point, backtrack to the first street right, **Calle Gran Canaria**, which leads us back to **Plaza Doctor Alfonso Spínola**.

If there's one route that you should walk on Lanzarote, this is it. Our route contains all the essentials for a top rate discovery and even the 280 metre ascent simply melts away as we climb a little-known donkey trail through the island's lushest vegetation. Originally a linear descent to **Haría**, we've now re-walked the route as an 'out and back' excursion, with basic refreshments taken at half way.

Short Route	**Stroll**
Take a taxi to **Bar/Rest Los Helechos** and walk the route as a linear descent to **Haría**.	Along the dirt road from **Haría**, as far as you like.

Access by bus:
N°7 from **Arrecife** calls at **Haría**; see appendices for details.

We start out from the centre of **Haría** outside **Bar Ney-Ha** on **Plaza de la Constitución** (Wp.1 0M) to go right in front of the *ayuntamiento* to stroll along to the **Eckholl** collection shop (Wp.2) where we go left on a small street lined with houses. It is gently uphill before going left to cross the stream bed and come up past a well (Wp.3) to a T-junction at the end of **Calle Angel**. Following the 'Deportivo' sign to the right, we start to leave the old village behind as we stroll along an avenue of palms.

Fields replace houses on our left as we pass César Manrique's house (Wp.4) on our right, shortly before the tarmac swings right (Wp.5) towards the sports complex. Here we continue straight ahead, the tarmac changing to dirt (Wp.6 12M) as we pass a ruined cottage to finally leave the housing behind.

Ahead, the line of the donkey trail which climbs the ridge at the end of the valley is clearly visible, the buildings on top of the ridge making for a rather daunting prospect from down in the valley. We stroll along through a bucolic landscape of black *picon* cultivated plots interspersed with fallow fields populated with endemic flora. Coming to a junction (Wp.7) we take the minor dirt road to our front right. Our gentle uphill stroll becomes more serious as the road steepens, becoming grassier as it ascends in a slogging ascent towards the main road. Where the dirt road swings left up to the tarmac we take a donkey trail straight ahead to climb up onto the road (Wp.8 27M).

Watching out for 'white knuckled' hire car drivers, we cross over onto the donkey trail's continuation on a long traverse across the slope. Endemic flora has narrowed the trail to path width as we climb up above a cultivated black *picon* plot which stands

Surrounded by plant life, far above Haría

A boulder-cobbled section of the trail

out amongst these long-abandoned terraces. At the end of the long climbing traverse, we come up to meet the main road again (Wp.9 40M) by the 'Val de Malpaiso' sign. Carefully over the road, we continue on the donkey trail in another climbing traverse. The plant growth on this steep hillside simply has to be seen to be believed; if you think of Lanzarote as 'grit and desert' then this floriferous setting will really surprise you. Giant sonchus, lavender, succulents and tamarisk cling to every available roothold.

A slogging ascent brings us up under massive buttresses which support the road, as a hairpin bend in the trail (Wp.10 43M) directs us towards another buttress. We come up to touching distance of the massive wall to zigzag steeply up alongside the tarmac (Wp.11) at a hairpin bend. Our trail, now mostly boulder-cobbled now, climbs steeply up through more zigzags to a hairpin bend (Wp.12) that directs us towards the **Mirador de Haría** building, a climbing traverse leading us up to the road again (Wp.13 48M). Carefully crossing the road, we find our trail's continuation 20 metres uphill where the path climbs up from a red rock dell, soon becoming boulder-laid again. As our trail curves right, we get views down the **Valle de Tenisía** as we push our way up through lush plant life to come up to the road again.

From here you could simply walk up the road to the Bar/Restaurant, but we cross the road to come onto the faintest section of the trail. Above us is a wooden cross which we use as a direction marker while climbing up over bare rock, before the trail resumes to take us past the cross (Wp.14). Twenty metres after the cross there is faint (easily missed) junction (Wp.15 55M), where our 'Capital Route' continues gently uphill to come onto a dirt road. At the junction we go left, to drop down the cobbled trail to the road (Wp.16).

Now it's an uphill stroll beside the crash barrier to turn into **Bar/Rest Los Helechos** (62M 570 metres), which may look closed from the road - but walk around the building to find a twee gift shop selling the usual tourist stuff and a large basic café geared up for the coach potato trade. It doesn't rate highly for refreshments, but it is a reasonably comfortable place to take a break and mix with the tourists and groups of lycra-clad cyclists who call in here.

Despite its unpromising name, **Malpaso** meaning 'bad pass/route', our new circular out of **Haría** is a Lanzarote classic combining the marvels of 'The Forgotten Trail'(Walk 28) with a hidden *barranco* stuffed with endemic flora and the possibility of seeing running water - a real rarity on Lanzarote. That's not all, add on the spectacular cliff-top views from **Mirador del Risco de Famara** plus a refreshment opportunity at another *mirador* - the scene is complete for a most memorable adventure.

It's longer, and tougher, than 'The Forgotten Trail' but still well within the compass of leisure walkers so if you only have time for one walk in the **Haría** region then make it our 'Barranco del Malpaso'; you won't regret it.

Access by car:
Either park in central **Haría** to follow the walk as described, or park at **Mirador del Risco de Famara** or **Restaurante Los Helechos** car parks to start our circular route at these options which give a unique view of our route and mid-walk refreshments in the centre of **Haría**.

Access by bus:
N°7 from **Arrecife** calls at **Haría**; see appendices for details.

We start out from the small square facing the *ayuntamiento* (town hall) in the centre of **Haría**(Wp.1 0M 294m) to stroll along the street (W) to the **Eckholl** shop (Wp.2 3M) where we turn left onto the **Calle Angel Guerra** to start heading away from the town (SW) passing a mixture of houses and plots as we come gently up to pass the sports ground (Wp3 12M) where the tarmac street becomes a dirt track. Past the last house, new-ish but not named, we are out into the countryside walking between stone walled fields and plots while ahead we have the great swoops of the LZ10 framing our return descent 'The Forgotten Trail'. It's easy strolling very gently uphill as we pass a section where a small stream has eroded the track down to trail width for a short section before we come up to pass a chained entrance on our right, followed by a chain across the main track just after it starts climbing up from the stream (Wp.4 21M 359m).

It's all been dreamily easy so far - but there's one tricky bit of wayfinding on this route and we are there now. Where the track moves away from the stream to run up past the chain into a large field (see Walk 26) there is no sign of any other route, but we need to follow the stream. After a few metres of stepping from stone to stone a trail emerges on the right side of the stream for us to snake up between stone walled terraces including vines. It's a narrow single-file path as it climbs above the watercourse for us to push past fennel and intense local endemics, passing another field of vines on our left before our path switches to the opposite side of the stream (Wp.5 30M).

As we climb through the endemic flora the terraces gradually change from cultivated to abandoned so reverting to nature. Water erosion has collapsed a terrace wall and narrowed the already narrow path requiring careful footwork. We're climbing steadily above the stream, negotiating another eroded section, to come onto stone steps which bring us up onto a broad dirt track (Wp.6 42M 444m) where suitably sized boulders provide convenient rest points before tackling the next climb up the *barranco* proper.

Ascending the *barranco*

What a difference a track makes; our earlier 'stream in a gully' has become a fully-fledged steep-sided *barranco* (signed 'Barranco del Malpaso'). We climb up the narrow stone path to pass two 'netted rock'dams, there to prevent flash flooding sweeping away the rich soil down in the valley floor. After the steep climb to the second dam (Wp.7) our path crosses the watercourse as a sharp turn in the *barranco* takes **Haría** from sight behind us as we climb steeply up past trees to come up to the remains of a cistern and hut which mark the upper reaches of the *barranco*. We continue upwards, cultivated fields appearing as the barranco finishes but our path continues uphill to a dirt track (Wp.8 60M 551m).

Across the track, our path continues up past stone-walled fields before swinging right to bring us onto another dirt track and the unexpected sight of picnic tables (Wp.9 66M 582m); after nearly three hundred metres of climbing ascent its almost as if divine providence has placed the tables here just for us. It's an easy stroll along (W) to meet the main track (Wp.10) where we turn left to follow the track uphill. You could clamber over the open ground to our west for views down the cliffs, but you'd be better advised to continue up the track, military camouflaged radomes coming into view as we reach the first access paths into the **Mirador del Risco de Famara Área Recreativa**.

Alternatively, continue on to the recreation area's car park (Wp.11 74M 615m). In Lanzarote's largest *área recreativa* you'll find a sizeable children's playground along with enough picnic tables to seat the largest of extended families, plus of course the *mirador*. Arrive here on a weekend and you'll find the place bustling with Lanzarote families settling in for a day's relaxation complete with catering; on weekdays you could have the whole place to yourself. Missing at any time are tourist hire cars; seemingly this spectacular location is too far from the tarmac for visitors to consider, much to their loss.

From the car park entrance we still have some gentle uphill along the broad track before we pass a dirt track accessing a building on our left and then come down to a crossroads where we swing left to pass a farm on our left before coming to the tarmac lane (Wp.12 97M) serving the **Ermita de las Nieves**. Our stroll along this section of high ground provides increasing views over the **Haría** valley and east to **Tabayesco**, and there's evidence of cultivation returning to this previously abandoned farming area in the form of new fields and farmhouses under construction. Along the tarmac (NNE) we come to a dirt track (Wp.13) accessing houses before we reach the main LZ10 road.

If you plan to call at **Restaurant Los Helechos**, recommended for its view rather than its cuisine, then continue down to the LZ10 and carefully walk along the main road to the extensive car park (wildly over-optimistic in size compared to the numbers who call here) (Wp.14 102M). Should you prefer to eschew the restaurant's delights then take the dirt track (N) on the route of Walk 30 to the path (Wp.13A) that leads down past the cross to the LZ10 with our return route on 'The Forgotten Trail' continuing across the road.

We always call in at **Restaurant Los Helechos**, really because it's there but also to marvel at this waste of a golden opportunity. At best it's a cafe and gift shop with a massive car park in a spectacular location, after which any description goes as rapidly downhill as the LZ10. Food and drink seem palatable enough but the café is a depressing monument to featureless formica which even the spectacular view from its windows can't lighten. Its gift shop is a marvel of everything that might possibly count as Lanzarote tat, seemingly displayed on the basis that the visiting 'coach potatoes' will buy anything no matter how awful.

On the descent

We return from **Los Helechos** (0M) on our 'Forgotten Trail' route, taking care on the section of road walking until we meet the donkey trail (Wp.15), then enjoying the wonderful descent, taking extreme care at the road crossings (Wps. 16, 17 & 18) to come out on a dirt track running along the valley floor into **Haría**.

We stay on the dirt track which becomes a tarmac street after passing the sports ground, then it's Ceasar Manrique's house before the houses form up into long terraces, all different so quite the opposite of UK terraced houses. Easy strolling down the street, passing a couple of side streets and through a wiggle, brings us back onto our outward route at a T-junction just a few metres from our start point in the plaza (Wp.19 45M).

The region around **Haría** contains quite a diversity of landscapes, ranging from lush valleys to barren hills and an unusual custom built *mirador* that nobody seems to know about. Our route is a complete mixture of a little tarmac, quite a lot of dirt road, a steep climb, a pathless section, breathtaking views; and the pleasure that comes from knowing that you wont have to share any of this with coach potatoes.

Stroll
From the **Eckholl** collection shop continue westwards on the street, which becomes the dirt road running up the valley to the *mirador* and return the same way.

Access by car:
Park in **Haría**.

Short Walk
Follow the route in reverse to the *mirador*, then continue on the dirt road back into **Haría**.

Access by bus:
N°7 from **Arrecife** calls at **Haría**; see appendices for details.

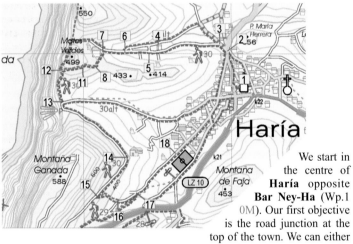

We start in the centre of **Haría** opposite **Bar Ney-Ha** (Wp.1 0M). Our first objective is the road junction at the top of the town. We can either walk straight up the **Máguez** road (N), or take the pedestrian street (E) past the church and then turn left (N) up the street; both options deal with the least pleasant part of the route as we slog up narrow streets. Both routes climb up the northern summit of the town, coming together at a junction (Wp.2) from which we head out on a country road on our front left (NE), **Calle Casa Atras**, rather a grand name for a smear of tarmac laid on a dirt road. Leaving the houses behind, we have views across the valley to a large quarry as we stroll down to a junction with a dirt road (Wp.3) going left (E).

Here we go left on the dirt road, though you could continue down the tarmac into the valley to go left on the next dirt road; it's a slightly longer and more energetic choice though, and with less extensive views. It's an easy stroll across the southern slope of the valley, passing through a patchwork of neatly cultivated plots and fallow fields being reclaimed by endemic plants.

We stroll past a squat house (Wp.4) surrounded by cultivated plots, and the dirt road becomes less used as we head up the valley. A steep dirt road drops down to the right linking our route with the longer alternative (Wp.5) before we crest a rise, then our road runs gently downhill to a junction with the alternative route (Wp.6). It is noticeable that the valley's southern slopes are more lush than the northern and mostly barren slopes, as we steadily ascend to come up to a breeze-block walled enclosure (Wp.7 33M).

Here we have another choice of route, our official route taking the faint track that climbs steeply up beside the enclosure. Another option is to continue on the dirt road to its end and follow a steep trail up over **Matos Verdes** to join our official route below the peak. The problem with this cliff top route is that it is usually extremely windy on all but the calmest days.

We take the faint track and start climbing steeply - and we do mean steeply - as the slope would benefit from having stairs cut into it.

The summit of the ridge, 40 minutes into the route

A 'puff and grunt' ascent takes us up past the top of the enclosure to reach the summit of the ridge by a gap in a stone wall (Wp.8 40M); after that exertion you have an excuse to stop and take in the extensive views over the **Haría** valley before continuing

Once through the wall, we swing right to follow it uphill towards a sad and lonely tree-stump, once a palm. The path is so little used we could think of this section as 'open ground' navigation. A small cairn (Wp.9) marks the spot where we move away from the wall and start to cross the long abandoned terraces to another gap in another stone wall (Wp.10). **La Caleta** and **Famara** come into view - and what a view it is - as we cross the terraces to a gap in another stone wall (Wp.11).

The path at 52 minutes

As we round the slopes below **Matos Verdes** we maintain altitude as we pass above a large stone storm-water wall which protects the lower valley, before coming to a path (Wp.12 52M) which runs down from the peak along the top of the cliffs; you'll notice that the wind's strength is multiplied several fold here near the cliff edge.

We pick our way down the path's gritty surface, which improves as we get lower, but it's still wiser to stop if you want to take in the impressive views. Our route runs down to join a dirt road beside an unusual structure (Wp.13 60M).

From above, this roofless structure resembles a very fancy grape vine cultivator, but from close to it is clearly a series of windbreaks for picnickers along with a parking area, so that they can enjoy the *mirador* views with some protection from the high winds; rather a shame that it does not feature on maps or in guide books, as visitors are most unlikely to stumble across this stunning location. While at the *mirador*, take the opportunity to look down the cliffs where you'll see a clear path cut across the cliff-face; though part of a Risco de Famara route, it's not recommended as the condition of this steep path is badly deteriorated.

From the *mirador* you have a choice of either short-cutting down the dirt road running down the valley to **Haría**, or taking our official longer route exploring the **Haría** valley. Leaving the *mirador*, we head up the dirt road which runs below the slopes of **Montaña Ganada**. After a steady uphill the gradient eases for easy strolling between abandoned terraces above and below our route, more of **Haría** coming into sight ahead of us.

Views over the Haría valley as we descend

A pungent whiff announces a goat farm ahead as we pass the first cultivated plots, climbing a rise before the road turns right above the goat farm (Wp.14 74M), giving excellent views over the **Haría** valley. Now it's easy strolling towards **Valle de Malpaso**, our route lined with gigantic prickly pear in places as we walk above neatly cultivated plots to come to a junction (Wp.15 80M).

Going left, we leave the main dirt track to descend between the plots on a rough track, once a boulder-laid donkey trail but now much eroded and covered in *picon* grit in places, requiring careful footwork on our descent. The track narrows to a trail and then to a path, before it comes down to a track which runs along the valley floor (Wp.16 88M).

Gratefully, we turn left and head along the track as it runs gently downhill to come onto a better stabilised track by a chained entrance (Wp.17 91M). It's comfortable strolling, crossing a plant-choked water course before we reach civilisation in the form of the sports centre football ground (Wp.18), after which the houses start. Continuing down the tarmac street we turn right at its end, by the **Eckholl** collection shop, and walk along to the **Plaza de la Constitución** and the prospect of an *agua con gas* followed by a cold beer in **Bar Ney-Ha** (110M).

31 CAPITAL ROUTE - HARÍA TO TEGUISE

In far distant days **Teguise** was the capital of Lanzarote, and as is the way of things, all routes led to the capital. This long linear route is a relic of those times, when it provided the main route from **Haría** to the capital. Being a ridge-top route, it has survived the depredations of road building largely intact, and its elevation produces many spectacular views. There's a stiff climb through Lanzarote's most floriferous landscape, but you can divert to **Bar/Rest Los Helechos** for refreshments after completing most of the ascent. Once on the ridge - more a wide-backed *lomo* - it's easy striding with stops to take in the awesome cliff-top views. After those views, trailing down into **Teguise** is rather disappointing, but at least it makes for easy walking.

Access by car:
Park in **Haría**.

Short Walk.
See Walk 28, 'The Forgotten Trail'

Access by bus:
N°7 from **Arrecife** calls at **Haría**; see appendices for timetables.

We start out from the centre of **Haría**, following the directions for 'The Forgotten Trail', up to Wp.15 (55M). If, with most of the ascent behind you, you want to take a break, then follow 'The Forgotten Trail' road walk up to **Bar/Rest Los Helechos**. On leaving the bar, walk south along the road and take the first tarmac lane off to the right to meet our official route just before the military radar golf-balls. From Wp.15 we continue straight ahead to come onto a dirt road. Keeping straight on along the track, we come up past a house, with **Bar/Rest Los Helechos** across a field on our left.

We walk up past two more houses, the radar golf-balls coming into sight, before a section of the track goes left while we continue onto the tarmac lane (Wp.16) which serves the **Ermita de las Nieves**. We have an easy stroll along the narrow lane, ignoring a track to our front right (Wp.17), and passing the radar station entrance (Wp.18), with views opening up to our left (E) over the main road and down to the coastal plain. Over a small crest, and now the *ermita* comes into view ahead of us.

The pilgrims' well in the *ermita*'s garden

This is easy striding country, so you might care to divert right to a *mirador* viewpoint at the top of the cliffs (Wp.19) before strolling over to arrive at the *ermita*'s walled courtyard (Wp.20 90M), where we take shelter from the wind inside its walled garden.

From the **Ermita de las Nieves,** our route could not be

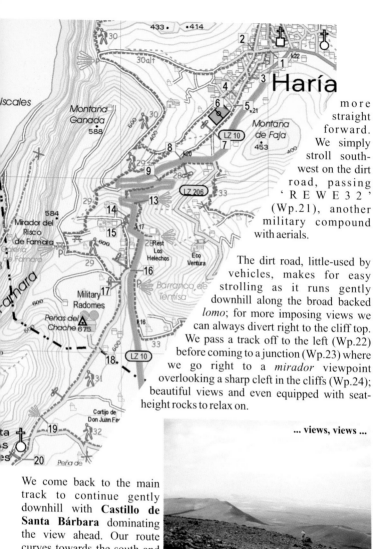

more straight forward. We simply stroll south-west on the dirt road, passing 'R E W E 3 2' (Wp.21), another military compound with aerials.

The dirt road, little-used by vehicles, makes for easy strolling as it runs gently downhill along the broad backed *lomo*; for more imposing views we can always divert right to the cliff top. We pass a track off to the left (Wp.22) before coming to a junction (Wp.23) where we go right to a *mirador* viewpoint overlooking a sharp cleft in the cliffs (Wp.24); beautiful views and even equipped with seat-height rocks to relax on.

... views, views ...

We come back to the main track to continue gently downhill with **Castillo de Santa Bárbara** dominating the view ahead. Our route curves towards the south and the first buildings of **Teguise** come into view.

A black *picon* field stands out against the barren landscape, just before a small uphill section, after which our track starts to run down off the *lomo* towards a patchwork of cultivated fields., then curving down to a cross-roads of tracks (Wp.25). The main road is away on our left as we go straight ahead on the narrower track running between the plots directly towards the town. We pass a track off to the right (Wp.26) before strolling up behind the first buildings of the town at a track junction (Wp.27) then reaching the football ground (Wp.28) where we finally come onto town streets. Keeping the church tower as our direction finder we stroll down the quiet streets (on weekdays at least) to arrive in the main square (Wp.29).

17th century **Ermita de las Nieves** (Chapel of the Snows) stands in isolation at Lanzarote's coldest, windiest and most exposed spot; visitors can shelter inside its surrounding walls, an oasis of relative calm away from the ferocity of the elements within which a garden thrives. Pilgrims of all sorts have paused here over the centuries, whether seeking spiritual sustenance or the quenching of thirst from its drinking water supply, though we can't vouch for its potability. The *ermita* itself is open on Saturdays (14.30 -18.00) and on 5th August, its Saint's day.

The views from the cliffs near the *ermita* shouldn't be missed, but take great care, especially on windy days (unfortunately, in the majority). **Playa de Famara** lies below, while the island of **La Graciosa** will be visible on a clear day to your right, beyond the **Risco de Famara** cliff. You may also make out the further islands of **Montaña Clara** and beyond that, **Isla de Alegranza** when visibility allows. The highest point on the island (670 metres) is **Peñas del Chache** to the north-north east, standing 70 metres higher than the *ermita* and occupied by a military installation, so is off limits to visitors.

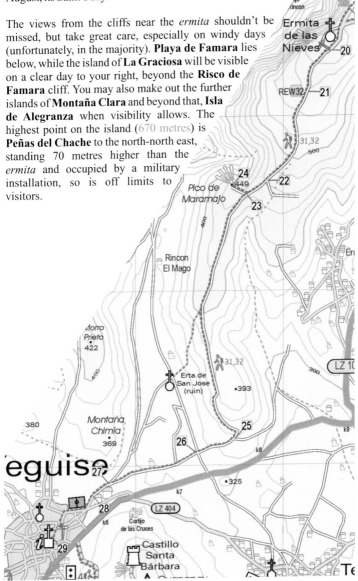

32 MALA TO TEGUISE

Another of Lanzarote's classic walking routes, all of which is on well stabilised dirt tracks or tarmac. The second half of the route, from **Ermita de las Nieves**, is common to Walks 31 and 32, so is not repeated again here. Our route has been only marginally affected by the LZ1 road which opened in March 2004 as our original track is now bridged over the new fast road. Our personal preference is for our **Haría-Teguise** route as the initial ascent simply melts away, but here it is always staring you in the face all the way up to the ridge. If you have an old Noel Rochford Landscapes (1998 edition) and a GPS, this is a good route to compare modern navigation techniques with a pre-GPS description.

Access by bus:
N°9, and some of the N°7 buses to **Mala**; alight at the *farmacía*, then walk along the old main road (N) for 200 metres and just past the village school our route starts at the tarmac lane on the left (Wp.1).

> **Short Walk**
> To **Ermita de las Nieves** and return (3½ hours) and you get the benefit from your climb on the downhill return.

Access by car:
2CSK Route (see P.17)
Not really a car driver's route except by our '2CSK' approach. Park off the old main road in **Mala**, but on the main road in **Teguise**; it's easier to find a car on the main road than in the warren of town streets.

Before starting out, it's a good idea to make sure you're equipped for this energetic climb up to the ridge. It's a long ascent of 2 hours plus and 600 metres, climbing almost every step of the way after a deceptively easy start. If you doubt your fitness, try routes 28 and 31 first.

From the old main road (Wp.1 0M) we walk up

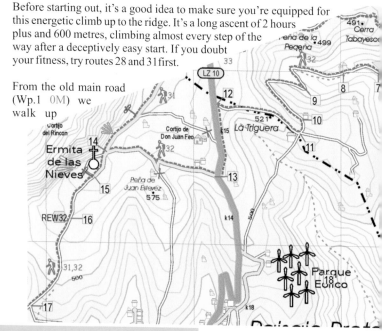

the tarmac lane, keeping right to pass in front of **Ermita de la Merceo** where our lane swings left to head across the plain towards the distant ridge. The new LZ1 road presents no difficulty as our route climbs gently up to a bridge over the new road (Wp.2), but the plethora of 'Armco' crash barriers and new wide dirt roads has ruined a once tranquil landscape. Over the bridge, and we are heading towards rural tranquility as we come up to a pair of houses at a junction and take the right hand track (Wp.3).

Cochineal farming

We're now climbing steadily up the side of a valley to go through a hairpin bend across its watercourse which gives us views back over our outward route, and the fields devoted to the 'tunera' cactus and their 'crop' of Cochineal beetle which are still cultivated in this region. We come up onto the line of the ridge and a junction beside a ruin (Wp.4 26M) where a track goes off to our right. There is still plenty of climbing to come, so you might want to take a break by walking out along the track to see the **Presa de Mala** dam, only containing water after wet weather.

From the *presa* junction we continue up the track toward a distant hamlet, the ground around our route deeply scarred by storm water erosion, in contrast to the massively walled terraces along this section. A steady ascent brings us up to the hamlet (Wp.5 44M) to walk past an impressive stone wall (Wp.6) and the radomes come into view; known locally as the 'golf balls'. With the cliff wall at the head of the **Barranco Valle del Palomo** looming ahead of us, we start slicing our route up into our 'one step after another' approach with a dam in the *barranco* floor (Wp.7) giving us the chance for a 'Look at that' breather. Passing a ruin (Wp.8) gives another excuse, as does a small bridge (Wp.9 71M). Cultivated plots enclosed by well built walls have relieved the ascent so far, but there is no denying that it is uphill and more uphill as our track zigzags up for us to reach a small house with an interesting back garden (Wp.10 88M).

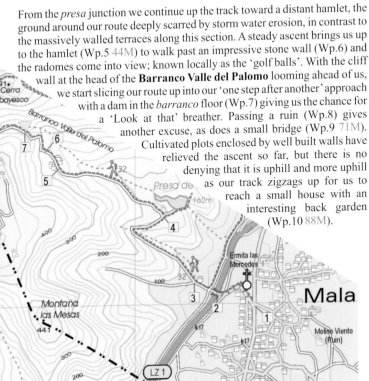

At last the gradient eases as we come up to a white building set alongside a five-way junction (Wp.11) to the north of the **Parque Eólico** wind farm. Turning right to pass in front of the building, we have the luxury of a gentle uphill stroll to come onto the LZ10 road (Wp.12 105M), facing the radomes set on **Peñas del Chache**. Turning left down the road we head towards the wind farm to take the lane on the right (Wp.13) signed to the **Ermita de las Nieves**. Up the lane, we wriggle through a zigzag before coming up to meet the dirt track of Walk 30 (Wp.14). Left up the tarmac, or around the dirt track that runs around the western side, brings us up to a well earned break at the island's best known *ermita* (Wp.15 132M).

Ermita de las Nieves (Chapel of the Snows) is a popular stopping off point for both walkers and drivers, and could be idyllic, if only someone would put in a little *tipico* bar to cater for the many visitors. Sitting on the well in the *ermita*'s courtyard is the most comfortable option, but we would not rely upon the it's water supply.

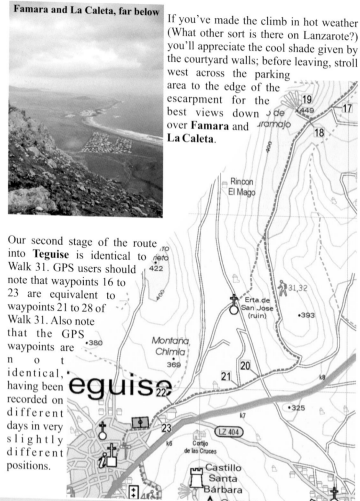

Famara and La Caleta, far below

If you've made the climb in hot weather (What other sort is there on Lanzarote?) you'll appreciate the cool shade given by the courtyard walls; before leaving, stroll west across the parking area to the edge of the escarpment for the best views down over **Famara** and **La Caleta**.

Our second stage of the route into **Teguise** is identical to Walk 31. GPS users should note that waypoints 16 to 23 are equivalent to waypoints 21 to 28 of Walk 31. Also note that the GPS waypoints are not identical, having been recorded on different days in very slightly different positions.

We usually avoid publishing routes that cross a lot of pathless open ground, but when John McDonnell suggested this circular based on **Tabayesco**, we realised it included an interesting trail we'd not seen before, along with a section of PRLZ01 official trail; it might be 'official' but it is largely pathless so that without a detailed walk description, and possibly GPS, innocents relying on the official signage could easily find themselves in difficulties.

As well as an interesting hike in its own right, with superb views, we now have the final parts of walking trails in this region giving us options to make our long linear routes out of **Haría** and **Mala** into circular routes. The pathless section at the start, if walked clockwise, will not be a problem for experienced walkers but if walked in reverse it is _vital_ that you keep going SW towards the red and white aerial after rounding **Cerro Tabayesco**; trying to head directly towards **Tabayesco** at this point is a disaster waiting to happen, in direct contrast to our 'easy and safe' route.

4/5   3H   11.5 km   500m / 500m   ↻   0*

* divert to **Restaurante Los Helechos** (2 star)

Access by bus:
Route Nºs 7 & 9 call at **Tabayesco** - see timetables at the back of the book.

Access by car:
From the LZ-1 turn off onto the LZ-206 to climb up to the start of **Tabayesco** where we park near the bus shelter and recycling bins at the start of the village.

Our start is on the dirt track alongside the recycling point (Wp.1 0M) that leads up to the Inalsa (Lanzarote's water authority) water tank. From here the least appealing terrain is the view SW up the naked steep hillside of a promontory that thrusts east from the **Famara** massif; yes, that is our first objective. On the premise that it's best to get the worst over first we set off up the Inalsa track where after 160 metres (Wp.2 3M) we go left onto the vague remains of a jeep track to start the serious ascent. Soon what remains of the jeep track disappears, for us to continue slogging over earth and small rocks with the occasional small rock outcrop on this gruelling ascent, relieved only by taking rest breaks to admire the increasing views.

On the dirt track at the start

Gradually we curve south-west (Wp.3 18M), following the promontory shoulder towards a large red and white aerial. After much huffing and puffing, we arrive amongst the restraining cables supporting the aerial (Wp.4 29M). On the bleak promontory beneath an oversized aerial mast is hardly a celebratory place but lets celebrate after that relentless 270 metre ascent as the worst, and it really is easily the worst, of our route is now behind us.

Now we indulge in the luxury of surveying our immediate route ahead. In the distance are the camouflaged radomes, while in front of us, the promontory runs down to its low point before rising up to the rocky outcrop of **Cerro Tabayesco** and another smaller outcrop on its right; the saddle between these two outcrops being our next destination. Looking carefully we can discern a faint trail running straight down (WNW) to the low point and then continuing uphill towards the saddle, the trail easier to see from above than when walking on some parts of it.

Heading downhill (WNW), we come onto the faint trail as it runs down beside shallow, long abandoned, terraces to the low point where the faint trail continues straight ahead in a steady ascent towards **Cerro Tabayesco**; if in doubt about the route simply continue heading for the largest rock outcrop. As we steadily approach the outcrop we come to a faint T-junction (Wp.5 40M) where we keep left to come up to the end of a jeep track alongside two remote cultivated plots nestling below **Cerro Tabayesco** (Wp.6 43M). This marks the end of the 'pathless open ground' navigation section of our route.

Note: if walking the route anticlockwise it is very important that you continue ESE at Wp.5, the right fork, and do not go left as we did the first time; it was not a pleasant experience.

The waypost at Wp.7

With all the difficult, pathless navigation and major ascent bits behind us, we can indulge in the luxury of relaxed walking while taking in the impressive views over the **Tabayesco** valley as we stroll along the track to the surprising sight of a PRLZ waypost (Wp.7 52M) at 459m altitude indicating that **Tabayesco** is 2.2km behind us; how the authorities know this is a mystery as we can't imagine any official who has followed our route (the only safe route) having the temerity to recommend it as an 'official PRLZ route'. The waypost is on a junction with a track forking left (SE) onto **Peña de la Pequeña** as we follow the main track downhill past a cabin and cultivated plots to another low point of the promontory, which also narrows so that as we climb up the track past ruins of cottages, we get views down onto our Walk 32 route climbing up the **Presa de Mala** valley. It's a rather steep ascent up the track to bring the radomes back into sight, as we come up to cultivated plots and cabins which we pass on our right as we approach the LZ-10 main road. Just as it seems we're going to step onto the road, our track turns right, paralleling the road for a short section before we step onto the tarmac (Wp.8 72M).

Normally we would walk on the left of a road, facing the oncoming traffic, but here we found it easier staying on the right to stroll past the 16km marker for the 500 metres that brings us to the *mirador* car parking and footpath (Wp.9 78M).

From the end of the *mirador* we cross over to walk on the left of the LZ-10 for the few metres before turning left onto the **Ermita de Las Nieves** lane and then immediately right onto the wayposted dirt track (Wp.10 80M) used by Walks 29 & 31. From here we simply follow the route of Walk 29 to take the trail off the track (Wp.11 86M) that leads down past the cross to cross the LZ-10 onto the 'Forgotten Trail' donkey trail, taking care on the road crossings, until we come to the last crossing of the LZ-10 (Wp.12 108M) where we leave the route of walks 28, 29 & 31.

On the LZ-10 we turn right, easiest to stay on the right of the road for the 400 metres downhill until we turn right onto the LZ-206 **Tabayesco** road (Wp.13 113M). Walking down the road, we step off onto a jeep track, accessing plots and a hut away on our left, just before the road's crash barrier starts. It is a picky descent on the rough track until it turns left, where we step off the track down two stone steps onto a narrow walking trail (Wp.14 117M). From the top of the trail we have superb views over the final section of our route from the bowl at the head of the valley, down to **Tabayesco** and the Atlantic Ocean. Our narrow trail winds its way steeply down into the head of the valley including a section of zig-zags before we emerge below the topmost cultivated plots on a dirt track (Wp.15 128M).

The track's continuation up the head of the valley is chained off as we turn left to head down the track, easy strolling after the slightly picky descent on that interesting trail, passing a farmstead's noisy dogs and chickens and a caravan holiday home. Ignoring minor tracks to left and right we arrive at a major track junction (Wp.16 137M) where we keep left following the valley's watercourse; if walking anticlockwise keep right at this junction otherwise you will find yourself climbing up to the LZ-206 far earlier than you expected.

Tabayesco near the end of our route

Our final section is easy strolling along the valley floor on the well-stabilised track, between a mixture of *malpais* and cultivated plots. Ignoring obvious side tracks, we pass a first house and two huts on our left, then a track left to a house hidden by trees before passing the last hut just before we come onto the end of a village street (Wp.17 155M).

From here, we keep straight ahead over a crossroads (village street right, dirt track left) to walk through the lower section of the village, coming gently uphill to emerge onto the LZ-206 opposite the bus shelter and recycling point (162M).

Whether you've diverted to the **Restaurant Los Helechos** or not, we recommend motoring down the LZ-206 to turn left onto the LZ-1. Then go round the 'thingy' roundabout to enter **Arrieta** and work your way through the streets to **Playa Garita** at the southern edge of **Arrieta**. Here we find a perfectly situated beach/promenade bar with plenty of parking (though very busy at weekends with locals) which should satisfy even the most discerning hiker's refreshment needs in a local *tipico* well off the tourist track.

This interesting circular route takes in bucolic farmland, upland meadows (yes, meadows), stunning cliff-top views, a peak and one of Lanzarote's most impressive *calderas*; only refreshments are missing. Ascents are never steeper than steady, and the range of landscapes and views makes even these seem relatively gentle. All the route is on either narrow tarmac lanes or well-stabilised dirt tracks, so you could drive this route - but why would you want to?

Some guides describe the main circuit of this route in the opposite direction. This involves a mind-sapping relentless ascent right from the start which makes the route seem more penance than enjoyment.

Stroll	Short route
Drive up the route in reverse and make the ascent of **Helechos** on foot	Omit the four diversions off the main circuit, though you'll miss some of the most interesting features.
	Alternative Short Route
	Park just off the **Guinate** road by Wp.6. Follow official route to Wp.9 and go right to return to your car - see map.

Access by car: with on street parking in **Máguez**.

Access by bus:
Nº7 runs from **Arrecife** to **Máguez**; see appendices for timetables.

We start off in the centre of **Máguez** by house Nº16 (Wp.1 0M) by going (ENE) along a quiet street past the church on our left to come along to a cross roads (Wp.2) where we go left. A steady uphill stroll takes us past houses and vegetable plots, with **Helechos** on our front left. The street gets steeper and narrower before we go over the crest to leave **Calle las Casillas** on a well-used dirt track (Wp.3 13M). After that steepish urban start we are now heading out (NE) into a bucolic landscape with the bulk of **Monte Corona** ahead of us. This is easy strolling between fallow and cultivated plots, passing tracks off to right and left, before coming to a junction (Wp.4 31M) where we go left on the minor track.

Our track gently climbs past a rock outcrop towards a pair of buildings. The buildings resolve into a house and its garage as we come to the crest of the track to see the main road and **Guinate** junction ahead of us. Another easy stroll down through a meadow landscape (yes, this *is* Lanzarote) brings us to the main road opposite the **Mirador de Guinate** road (Wp.5 39M).

Along the **Guinate** road, we turn off the tarmac onto a track (Wp.6 41M). Now it is a steady climb round the slopes of **Helechos**, the effort partly relieved by the expanding views as we ascend past ancient walls and long abandoned plots. Past a cultivated field and a lichen-encrusted outcrop announces our arrival at a pass (453 metres) and a few metres further (Wp.7 50M) we take a diversion to our right to follow a faint track (NW) to a viewpoint (Wp.8 52M) at a stone wall overlooking the **Guinate** valley. Just beyond the wall, stone-walled, black *picon* plots of grape vines contrast with the meadows we've crossed.

The purple sheen of Viper's Bugloss

Back on the main track (Wp.7) we head up (WSW) through the waving grassland and meadow flowers towards another pass. Viper's Bugloss flowers give the slopes a gentle purple sheen as we come up to overlook the **Valle de Guinate**: the dirt road running along the valley is the route of our Alternative Short Walk. Now we stroll along overlooking the valley beside fallow meadow fields. On our front right is a remarkable 'bite' out of the ridge as though bitten by giant teeth; yes, you <u>could</u> drive this route, but how much more enjoyable to stroll through this wonderful landscape.

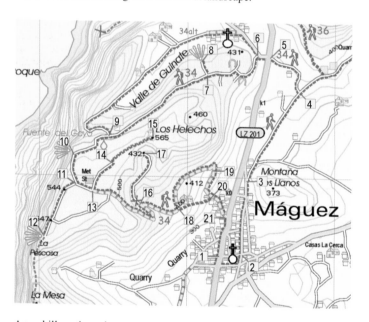

An uphill section takes us up past a house to a junction (Wp.9 74M), where our Alternative Short Route goes right to drop down towards the valley floor.

Just past the junction we pass a pair of pits beside the track before reaching a Y-junction where we take the left fork; the two tracks soon coming together again. A valley drops steeply down on our right as we continue uphill to the top of the cliffs (Wp.10 82M); take care if you approach the cliff edge as the winds are powerful. We stay on the track as it undulates along (SE) away from the cliffs to reach a junction (Wp.11 87M). Here we take the minor track (WSW) heading for the cliff tops at **La Pescosa**. We walk up past fields cut out of the meadows to come up onto the headland.

This track ends at a storm-eroded area (Wp.12 97M) from where we take in impressive views down over **El Risco de Famara** to **La Caleta** and the plain beyond.

Back at the main track (Wp.11 107M) we head (E) past a white meteorological station, where the track becomes tarmacked, to another junction (Wp.13 111M) where a track goes left (N). Taking to the track for our third diversion off the main circular route, we climb up onto a broad backed ridge which although only a few metres above our earlier route is almost barren with the exception of a black *picon* field. We walk along the rough track to swing left and right beside the field (Wp.14 117M).

Ahead, the track leads us up the slope to the transmitter hut sitting on the top of **Helechos**, views opening up down over the **Valle de Guinate** from the saddle before the final walk up to the hut (Wp.15 125M).

David just visible on the Helechos peak track

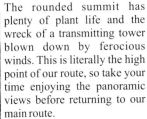

The rounded summit has plenty of plant life and the wreck of a transmitting tower blown down by ferocious winds. This is literally the high point of our route, so take your time enjoying the panoramic views before returning to our main route.

Back on the tarmac (Wp.13

The *caldera* below Helechos peak

139M) we head (E) downhill, steadily at first and then steeply down through a hairpin bend to a junction (Wp.16 148M) where a track heads off towards the **Helechos** peak from the second hairpin bend. By now you might well be dreaming of a cold beer in **Máguez** and be tempted to ignore this track, but stay with us for our fourth, and final, diversion off the main route. We walk out along the track, which is nothing special until it reaches a crest for us to find ourselves looking down into the *caldera* directly below the **Helechos** peak.

Our track continues down around the wall of the crater to reach the flat floor at the foot of sheer cliffs (Wp.17 155M), giving us an impressive sense of scale in this soaring cliff landscape despite some rubbish dumping. Climbing back up the track out of the *caldera*, we arrive back at the tarmac. Now the return to **Máguez** is straightforward, as we simply walk down the tarmac lane, descending past cultivated fields, a farm (Wp.18 170M) and an unusual dwelling set below the road (Wp.19); our preference is to walk the lane but at Wp.18 a trail is signed downhill which rejoins the lane at Wp.20.. Houses start (Wp.20) shortly before we meet the main road (Wp.21) where we go right to walk down to our start point.

A pleasing rural route, giving close up views of Lanzarote's agricultural region seldom seen by the average visitor. The range of different landscapes encountered has to be seen to be believed.

Originally this was a linear route finishing in **Yé** but as the village is only served by two buses a day, and having our **Montaña Corona** route nearby (Walk 36), we've combined old and new routes to produce a pan-handled circular route based on **Máguez**; with a shorter car based alternative from **Yé**. At 15kms, this is one of our longer routes but the easy walking for most of the route results in a comparatively low exertion rating.

| 3 | 4 H | 15 km | 340m / 340m | ! | ↻ | 2* |

Short Route
Park in **Ye**'s extensive church car park then walk along the LZ-201 (E) for 150 metres to join the main route at Wp.14, following the walk description to arrive at Wp.22 on the dirt track where we then follow the track NE to Wp.6 to follow the main walk description from Wp.6 to 14 to arrive back in **Yé** at our start point.

*in the **Centro Social Cultural de Yé**
though they're not always open

Access by bus:
Route N°7 runs approx. 2-hourly from **Arrecife** to **Máguez**. See timetables for details.

Starting from the centre of **Máguez**, we follow the same route as Walk 34, 'Helechos Circular' until that route turns left at Wp.4 (31M). At this junction we keep straight ahead (NE) on the main track to walk gently uphill, as the bulk of **Monte Corona** starts to loom over us. Passing a water tank with blue door we come over a rise by a second water tank (Wp.5 37M) to come into a *picon* landscape, much harsher than the earlier plain. Sturdy boulder walls criss-cross the land ahead as we pass a *picon* quarry, very different to the cultivated fields away on our right.

Torrecilla de Domingo

Views over the Vega Grande valley

As our track wriggles through the moonscape, the top of the large mansion of **Torrecilla de Domingo** comes into view, gradually revealed as we come alongside cultivated plots and keep left at a junction, just before meeting the main road (Wp.6 57M).

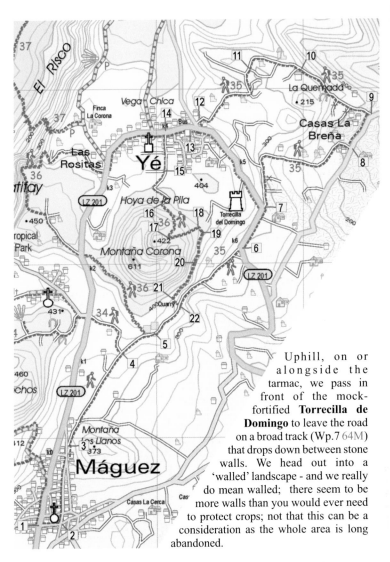

Uphill, on or alongside the tarmac, we pass in front of the mock-fortified **Torrecilla de Domingo** to leave the road on a broad track (Wp.7 64M) that drops down between stone walls. We head out into a 'walled' landscape - and we really do mean walled; there seem to be more walls than you would ever need to protect crops; not that this can be a consideration as the whole area is long abandoned.

We stay on the main track, passing two tracks off right before coming over a rise, where the landscape ahead becomes more normal with cultivated plots. Strolling down the track, we pass a weekender cottage followed by cultivated *picon*-covered plots and houses as our route runs down to the **Orzola** road (Wp.8 90M). Going left (NE) we stroll down the road to take a track (Wp.9 95M) off to the left that curves around behind a clutch of modern houses.

Our route climbs up towards the twin peaks of **Montaña Quemada** which we pass on our left as the track rises up to overlook the **Vega Grande** valley. With the views comes a stiff uphill section of the track, stone-walled on our left and with a steep drop on our right, which lasts until we reach the saddle at an art-deco house (Wp.10 109M).

Over the saddle, we ignore a minor track left as we head down above cultivated fields in the valley below us, passing an old mill and a ruin beside interesting rocks before reaching cultivated fields which stretch up the valley on our right. Passing a track off to the left (Wp.11 120M) and one off to the right, we face a stiff climb up from the valley floor, passing another two tracks off to the left before the gradient eases beside walled grape vines.

Passing a house on our left, we walk steadily uphill in a slogging ascent to the first houses of **Yé** (Wp.12 133M).

The Centro Socio de Yé

On the LZ-201 main road, we turn right (W) to call in for refreshments at a most unusual tipico, the **Centro Socio Cultural de Yé** (Wp.13) beside the main bus stop for coffee and to admire the murals - the *centro* welcomes visitors but has been closed (no notice or information available) on our last two visits to **Yé**.

Continuing along the main road we pass a street of to our left before coming to a dirt track (Wp.14 141M) where we join the route of Walk 36 Corona's Northern Tour by taking the dirt track (S) gently uphill through a *zoco*-cultivated area. Cultivation gives out (Wp.15) as we continue gently uphill, ascending through lazy zigzags until our track runs out close to the mountain base (Wp.16 153M). From here we take a walking trail that continues up past the last *zocos* to a stately palm where the ascent steepens through endemic plant life, passing a trail on our right before going through a stone wall to continue up to the edge of **Montaña Corona**'s *caldera* (Wp.17 165M) - see Walk 36 warning.

From the *caldera* we head west to follow an old stone wall, clambering from level to level through the vigorous plant life on a pathless decent before we drop down onto an old terrace where a faint path brings us to a metal fence (Wp.18 177M) where a very broad stone wall goes right (SE). We go right onto the top of the stone wall for seventy metres before stepping down onto a narrow walking trail (Wp.19). our narrow trail passes through abandoned *zocos* before contouring round the mountain, the narrowness of the trail combined with cutting across the steep *picon* slope might give problems for vertigo sufferers until we reach a section of volcanic boulders (Wp.20).

Past the boulders, our path is much less vertiginous as it takes us steadily downhill to the '*picon*-cliff' edge of an old quarry (Wp.21). Here our path turns down by the edge of the quarry in a steep, skittery, slippery decent on loose *picon* grit - consider going down on hand feet and bottom; undignified but safe - to drop us onto the dirt track of our outward route (Wp.22 199M). From here we have an easy stroll (SW) along the track for two kilometres to join the lane north of **Máguez** from where we have another kilometre of street walking back to our start point.

Approach the north of Lanzarote and one thing stands out - **Montaña Corona**, the classic volcanic cone peak that dominates the view ahead as you leave **Máguez**. We have great routes in the north (see walks 34, 35 and 37) but somehow we'd never tackled the big northern mountain. Then came the happenstance of meeting Carmen Portella Ernest through Andreas at the **Bike Station** who invited us to join her group on a recently pioneered route taking in the mountain's *caldera* and **Famara** views as part of a northern tour. Carmen, a professional guide, pioneered this route; this, and the prospect of convivial walking companions combined with **Montaña Corona** was an opportunity too good to miss. As Carmen, surprisingly, did not know of the social centre theatre and bar in **Yé** (see Walk 35) we planned to add this surprise refreshment stop ending to the expedition.

The result is an interesting route taking in some amazing sights though as a new route paths are not the clearest and there is a risk of vertigo on the narrow path curving round below the peak.

*in **Centro Social Cultural de Yé**
though they're not always open

Short Walk A
Yé church to **Corona Caldera** and return (2 walker, 3kms, 1 hour).

Short Walk B
Famara cliffs and return, park on Camino de Guatifay and follow route to Wp.16 and return (2 Walker, 2.5kms, 1 hour).

Access by car:
Park in **Yé** church's extensive car park - avoid religious fiestas (not feasible by bus).

We start from the church car park entrance (Wp.1 0M) to walk along the road (E) for 150 metres where we take a dirt track (Wp.2 4M) heading (S) towards the mountain. Our track winds gently uphill through a *zoco*-cultivated area, grapes and almonds, side tracks accessing the fields as we steadily close with

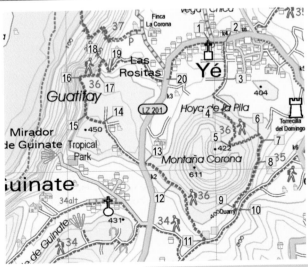

Montaña Corona. Gradually, cultivation gives out (Wp.3) as we continue gently uphill through abandoned fields and a shallow valley before ascending through lazy zigzags until our track runs out close to the mountain base (Wp.4 16M). A walking trail continues up past the end of the *zocos* to a stately palm where our narrow trail starts a more serious ascent through endemic plant life, passing a trail coming in from our right before going through a stone wall to continue up to the edge of the mountain's *caldera* (Wp.5 28M).

.. an impressive *caldera* ..

It's an impressive *caldera*, the cone's southern section intact as seen in the view from **Máguez**, while the northern rim has collapsed giving us a 'rim-edge' view down to the caldera floor - don't go too close to the edge as the rocks are undercut - more collapses can be expected at any time! From the *caldera* we head west to follow an old stone wall. There's no path as such as we negotiate abandoned terraces, clambering from level to level through, and round, the vigorous plant life including prickly pear! Don't think it's all like this; we're on the worst section of the route - as more walkers beat a path down beside the wall a reasonable walking trail will emerge.

Finally we drop down an old terrace onto a faint path that brings us to a metal fence (Wp.6 40M) where a very broad stone wall goes right (SE). There is an onward path, but we go right onto the top of the broad stone wall for seventy metres before stepping down onto a narrow walking trail (Wp.7).

Our trail winds through an area of abandoned *zocos* before contouring round **Montaña Corona**. It's a narrow one-person path cutting across steep *picon* slopes which might give problems for vertigo sufferers until we come to a section of volcanic boulders and *vinagrera* plants (Wp.8). Past the boulders, we continue our gradual descent on the narrow *picon* path to arrive at the 'picon-cliff' edge of a quarry (Wp.9). Our path turns down by the edge of the quarry for a steep, skittery, slippery descent on the loose picon grit - consider going down on all fours (undignified but safe) while the adventurous might consider a 'scree-surf' descent to the quarry floor; both options bring us down onto the dirt road (of Walk 35, Wp.10 62M).

On the trail after **Wp.11**

After the narrow path this road is luxury; we stroll along to a pair of water cisterns set below the southern slopes of **Montaña Corona** (Wp.11 70M). Carmen declared a break at this point. We all consume the packed snack lunches she's provided, while showing us the cisterns' construction and explaining their key role in local agriculture.

From the top of the second cistern (Wp.11 0M) we take a very faint trail heading up over the *picon* (NW) towards a saddle below the slopes of the mountain. From the saddle we walk up through an old terrace wall as we head towards a dark lava rock wall; it's easy uphill open ground walking but there's no defined path as we cross old terraces to step above the lava rock wall (Wp.12 15M). Here we walk above the wall, which reduces to nothing as we continue uphill across another wall to come onto a *picon* walking trail; following this brings us above another small quarry where we have another slip/slidey descent to come onto the road facing **Camino de Guatifay** (Wp.13 27M).

.. views ..

Carefully crossing the road we stroll up the **Camino de Guatifay** dirt road with views down over **Guinate** and the **Tropical Park** while passing a couple of houses on our left, complete with a 'Cliffs de Guinate' sign, before we come to a white cottage on our right, just past which a dirt track goes right while we turn left (Wp.14

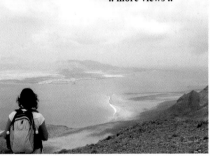
.. more views ..

38M) on an old track, now bouldered against vehicle access, to head directly towards the cliffs.

As we've been walking only gently uphill since the road, the top of the **Famara** cliffs and the views (Wp.15) come on us suddenly - a pleasant 'suddenly' as the views are stupendous.

Swinging right, we walk gently downhill with **Las Salinas** and the island of **Graciosa** laid out below us, to pick up a cliff-top path (about four metres in from the edge); take your time on this section as the views, firstly back along the cliffs to the **Guinate** *mirador* and later (Wp.16 52M) over **Las Salinas** and **Graciosa** are some of Lanzarote's best - though remember to 'Stop, and look at the view'. Our route swings right (E) along the line of the cliffs over rough ground to step over a low wall (Wp.17) then swings left on a narrow walking trail descending towards fields in the valley floor.

Where the path goes over a wall (Wp.18) to continue towards **Las Salinas** *mirador*, we go right to double back and descend towards the fields and a grey/blue gate. After crossing a gully on a 'cable-drum' bridge we pass the gate to come onto a dirt track (Wp.19 64M).

The church at our start/finish (Wp.1)

It's an easy stroll along the dirt track which winds along the floor of a small valley literally stuffed with endemic flora until we come up to a house with noisy dogs (chained) at the junction with the road (Wp.20 76M). Striding out up the road, watching for traffic, we pass the outlying houses of **Yé** as we close with our start point at the church parking area (Wp.1 85M).

We haven't passed any opportunities for refreshment around the whole route so we could try our Walk 35 unusual *tipico* at **Yé** social centre; just continue along the road (E) towards the centre of the village - as much as the village has a centre - to the bus stop where we find the social centre. Inside is a theatre setting with wall murals and a café, and when we've found it open on all previous visits we were assured that all visitors will be most welcome - though a little bit of Spanish helps. This time, with Carmen and the walking tour in tow, we found the centre shut - most disappointing, though we hope this most unusual of Lanzarote *tipicos* will be open and welcoming when you call in.

Yé is a sleepy farming village far removed from the excesses of Lanzarote's beach resorts. In addition to its rural tranquility, it boasts the most unusual *tipico* bar on the island in the **Centro Socio Cultural de Yé** alongside the main bus stop; do call in for coffee and admire the wall murals. Most visitors who discover **Yé** are simply passing through on their way to the 'pay on entry' sanitised **Mirador del Río**; once a simple gun emplacement dating from the civil war, but now upgraded to a 'tourist' attraction for the coach potatoes.

Less well known and largely undiscovered by the casual visitor is the *mirador* overlooking the **Salinas del Río**, where you'll not only enjoy similar views, but you'll be in the unusual situation of seeing your whole walking route laid out in front of you before you start out. Even if you don't plan to walk the **Salinas del Río** walk, you must visit this *mirador* if your visit to Lanzarote is to be complete.

Access by car (not feasible by bus):
From **Máguez**, drive past the **Guinate** junction, and turn off the main road 1.7 kilometres further on, onto a narrow lane at **Las Rositas**. Drive carefully down the lane until the imposing **Finca La Corona** is on your right, and then turn left onto a stone-flagged road which widens into a car park.

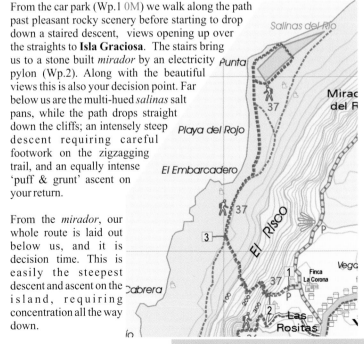

From the car park (Wp.1 0M) we walk along the path past pleasant rocky scenery before starting to drop down a staired descent, views opening up over the straights to **Isla Graciosa**. The stairs bring us to a stone built *mirador* by an electricity pylon (Wp.2). Along with the beautiful views this is also your decision point. Far below us are the multi-hued *salinas* salt pans, while the path drops straight down the cliffs; an intensely steep descent requiring careful footwork on the zigzagging trail, and an equally intense 'puff & grunt' ascent on your return.

From the *mirador*, our whole route is laid out below us, and it is decision time. This is easily the steepest descent and ascent on the island, requiring concentration all the way down.

Contemplating the descent

Concentrating on where you are putting your feet helps combat any sense of vertigo, as does facing the cliff when taking breaks. However if it is windy, or any sign of bad weather, we would suggest you save this route for another day.

On the zigzag descent

We set off, stepping down through the small, steep zigzags in a near vertical descent. This continues down for over a hundred metres before there is any relaxation on a moderate slope, and then we tackle a second series of small, steep zigzags for another hundred metres of near-vertical descent.

Finally, our trail comes to a steady descent and passing a fainter trail going left, we keep straight on. Easy walking brings us down to a T-junction with a track (Wp.3 48M).

Having made the descent, we are now free to explore the beach and salt pans, either by keeping to the track (N) or using the tracery of small paths that have been walked. The track ends at an electricity transformer that sends power over to **La Graciosa** via a sea bed cable. **Salinas del Río** is no longer in production, but at least its 'pans' are still here, and the evaporating sea water creates some beautiful colours. Cozzie-optional swimming is popular at the beach of **Playa del Risco**, so do indulge yourself if you wish. This is a beautiful isolated region, where we usually see only eco-responsible walkers, so it's an unwelcome surprise to find so much litter, in particular broken bottles, detracting from its natural beauty.

At some stage we have to remember that civilisation in the form of our car is at the top of that cliff. Personally we prefer the ascent to the knee-jarring descent despite its 'puff & grunt' nature requiring a lot of recovery stops, but like it or hate it, it has got to be climbed. At least, when we get back to the *mirador* we certainly have a well-earned sense of achievement.

El Risco de Famara provides a dramatic backdrop to this easy route along the base of the cliffs before descending to beach level and returning on an easy track. Easy that is, if the wind is not blowing. **Famara** is famous for its wind and when it blows, this easy beach-side walk is transformed into a struggle through a desert sandstorm. If you walk this route in the morning, then the first half will be shaded by the tall cliffs. The earlier you start, the shadier the route is - much more refreshing than walking in the blazing intensity of the afternoon.

*in complex and La Caleta

Access by car:
Park on the roadside just before reaching **Famara** bungalow development.

Access by bus:
Nº20 from **Arrecife** offers a limited service to **Caleta de Famara**; see appendices for timetables.

From the corner of the **Famara** development (Wp.1 0M) we head up the private road (SE) on an easy stroll past the walled squat bungalows. Ahead and above are the golf ball radomes on a ridge behind the main **Famara** cliffs as we come up to a sign for the reception (Wp.2). From here you could continue ahead, signed 'playa', to skirt the development, but our choice is to go left (NE) to walk between the square bungalows with curved walls. Past the reception, bar and shop, we reach the far side of the development (Wp.3 12M) where we go right (SE) to walk uphill, going right and left at the top of **Calle Aguamala** to come up between the houses and meet the beach road just beyond a barrier (Wp.4 17M). Interesting to note the change in architectural style between the lower and higher bungalows; below reception are square houses with curved walls, while above reception, the houses are curved with straight walls.

Going left on the broad dirt track (NE), we're back to easy strolling as we come down past little gobbets of lava rock beside the route; insignificant beside the impressive cliffs, but nevertheless large rocks in their own right. When the main track swings towards the beach (Wp.5 25M) - a short stroll option - we continue straight ahead on a steady ascent that brings us up to pass an old restored farmstead (Wp.6 27M), and on our right a

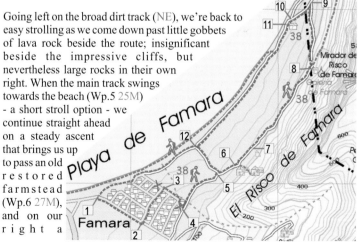

cobbled trail leads up to a second house and its veritable oasis of a walled garden amongst this barren wilderness. Along the track, we pass a walled threshing circle before coming below an old ruin (Wp.7), the track getting rougher as we ascend. It is steadily uphill towards an intriguing white building that peeks out from behind the ridges which run down from the towering cliffs. As we move along below the cliffs, the surroundings become more floriferous, the slopes becoming covered in *tabaiba* and other endemic plants; even the giant dandelion-like *sonchus* thrives here, showing that this is a 'wet' area compared to the barren land earlier in the route.

Round a small headland, the house comes back into view, a large spoil heap giving a clue as to what lies ahead. We come up beside the little house (Wp.8 47M 136 metres) to find that it sits at the entrance to a tunnel into the cliffs. In this unusual elevated position we

Wonderful views from the spoil heap

.. the aquamarine sea crashes onto rock 'pimples' ..

can appreciate both the towering cliffs and the beach curving around to **La Caleta**. A track leads up behind the house past an old white water tank (NNE), while down below us beside the beach track stands a white building which is our next destination.

We take the downhill track behind the house (N), more a path than a dirt road with a rubble-ised surface requiring careful footwork. As we pick our way down, the aquamarine sea crashes onto rock 'pimples', and the beach raises its own sea mist. Our track becomes increasingly rubble-strewn as we pass a steep path down to our left, a possible short cut to miss a loop of the track, while we stay on the track to drop down to a junction (Wp.9 60M). Going left (SW), we continue dropping down towards the white building on the rubble-strewn track. Passing the lower end of the short cut path, we pick our way down to a junction (Wp.10) with the *playa* track. At last we're back to comfortable strolling towards the old pumping house and a beach-side pillbox (Wp.11 68M).

The final section needs hardly any description. You could walk along the pebble beach, but our choice is to take the *playa* track for an easy stroll (SE). Easy that is, if it isn't windy, when it can be more like fighting our way through a desert storm than an easy stroll. When the *playa* track swings inland (Wp.12), keep straight ahead on a minor track (SE) which almost peters out before reaching the corner of the bungalows. Here, you could cut through the houses or keep to the sand dunes and beach before curving round the beach side of **Famara** to come onto the road near your car (100M).

39 CALDERA BLANCA

We've saved the best for last - not that it was the last route walked and 'best' is our personal opinion - which includes experiencing the 'lava sea' followed by climbing the crater rim of the *caldera* along with a surprising sight to go with superb views from the rim. There are no refreshments (a short drive away) but then, no route is completely perfect!

This is one of the new routes encouraged by the island government, who have opened up and improved the path through the lava sea to reach the **Caldereta** and **Blanca** *calderas*; previously you could only approach them from the north after a lengthy off-tarmac drive which would negate your hire car insurance, so more congratulations to the authorities for encouraging walking through improved access.

Walking along the crater rim, we overlook steep (very) slopes down to the floor of the *caldera* which might upset vertigo sufferers - and only undertake this route in good weather conditions - dry and with low windspeeds.

Access by car:

Depending from which direction you arrive, you'll be looking for the LZ67 road signed to 'Visitors' Centre'. Normally you'll be turning off the LZ56 main road in **Mancha Blanca**. As you leave **Mancha Blanca** houses behind, look for a tarmac lane on your right, after which you want to take the next dirt track on your right. If you reach a tarmac lane on your left you've gone too far; if you reach the **Visitors' Centre** you've gone way too far. Take the dirt track, easily driveable, to its end at a small parking area for a dozen cars and a 'Caldera Blanca' (official walk number 4) signboard. If the parking area is full go back to **Mancha Blanca**, park and walk in; don't park on the dirt track as it is in regular use by farmers.

From the end of the car park (Wp.1 0M) we continue on the track, bouldered against vehicle access, which in a few metres peters out for us to come onto the new path cut through the lava field. While the path is well made, just look each side to see what conditions would be like without it. It is mighty stony underfoot giving us a rocking gait as we slowly progress towards **Caldereta** which shields the bulk of **Montaña Blanca** from this viewpoint.

Any thoughts that this is a calm lava sea are dispelled as we drop into a valley formed between waves of lava - it's quite surreal to think that this was molten magma that set into the shapes we now see. After winding across the floor our path climbs out of the valley into a seriously disrupted landscape of peaks and holes like an angry sea frozen in rock formations. Our path guides us through this wild barren landscape to a junction (Wp.2 18M), the path to our right having stones across it; keeping to the main path, we snake our way through the lava, passing a small tree growing in the centre of the path, unusual in this barren waste. As we curve around the north of **Caldereta** we leave the lava sea (Wp.3 25M) for the luxury of a dirt path and flower-bedecked slopes (in February) as we come up to the entrance to **Caldereta** (Wp.4 31M). Just a few steps off the main trail brings us to the view into the *caldera*; and what looked like a small cone compared to **Montaña Blanca** is a most impressive sight; from the entrance there's a tempting option to follow a steep path ascending to the *caldera*'s rim. Back on the main trail, we climb steadily until, approximately half way up **Caldereta**, our trail turns to cross the lava (Wp.5). If the previous lava was an angry sea, then this is a furious torrent of tortured rock trapped between two volcanic cones; after the manicured paths so far we're now on bare pathless rock, following cairns for our route across the torrent; if in doubt about the route then scan ahead for the next cairn before heading off.

.. flower-bedecked slopes ..

After twisting, turning and clambering from cairn to cairn we're across the lava to come onto a dirt path (Wp.6 42M) and a junction where we go right so that in thirty metres we are angling up towards the **Caldera Blanca** rim from beside a loose rock shelter. A traverse across the slope on the faint worn path, including going through a rock channel, brings us up onto the lowest point of the crater rim (Wp.7 55M) to find that it consists of a broad top up to five metres wide, before it rolls off to near vertical slopes dropping to the *caldera* floor.

Surprisingly, the floor of the *caldera* way below us is covered in abundant vegetation, a direct contrast to the landscape outside the volcanic cone. What we first take to be dots resolves into a large flock of goats apparently enjoying the rich grazing found in this verdant and unlikely oasis.

Buoyed by the views, we set off up the great curving slope of the rim towards the summit, the views expanding over the southern lava fields as we climb while to the north over the crater rim we look out over the lava and **Montaña Teneza** to the Atlantic Ocean.

The first third of the ascent is easy uphill walking until we come to wind-sculpted rock ledges providing amphitheatre style seating when we take a break (Wp.8 75M). Now the climbing becomes more serious as we climb from ledge to ledge before the final ascent on the narrowing rim to the summit cairn and trig point (Wp.9 89M 468m). The views

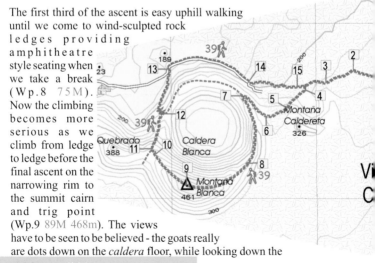

have to be seen to be believed - the goats really are dots down on the *caldera* floor, while looking down the

.. the caldera way below us ..

southern face we find that Lanzarote's outdoor artists have been at work creating giant footprints and a huge mouse/rat from lava rocks at the base of the mountain. From the summit the only way is down as we carefully pick our way around the western rim to come down onto a goat trail whose loose surface

On the summit (Wp.9)

again needs careful concentration before a path finally emerges (Wp.10) to take us down to the saddle between **Montaña Blanca** and **Risco Quegrado**. Down on the saddle we pick up the path (Wp.11 115M) running between the two volcanic cones as an alternative to picking our way down the rocky nose of the *caldera* rim.

Down below it is surprising to see so many cultivated fields on the *islotes* (islands) set amongst the lava sea. Our path follows the rim until we come to a zigzag descent (Wp.12) down the western slope on the remains of a stone-laid donkey trail. At the end of the zigzags we are onto a 'normal' dirt walking trail interspersed with tricky rock sections running down to meet with a dirt track (Wp.13). Now we are into relaxed walking round the northern base of the *caldera* to pick up the path across the lava (Wp.14) just below some newly constructed corrals at the end of dirt track. Now it is back onto a rocking gait until we come to the far side of the lava 'torrent' (Wp.15) just after which we meet up with our outward trail.

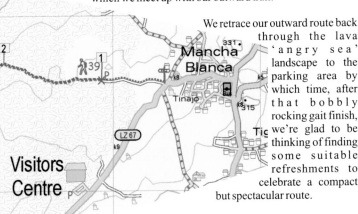

We retrace our outward route back through the lava 'angry sea' landscape to the parking area by which time, after that bobbly rocking gait finish, we're glad to be thinking of finding some suitable refreshments to celebrate a compact but spectacular route.

Having pioneered the first published walking route for this previously unknown region, 'The Hidden Barrancos', in our Lanzarote Walking Guide 1995, it's very pleasing to see an increasing number of walkers discovering these landscapes. By the time we produced Walk! Lanzarote (2004), new refuges had been built on the route overlooking **Barranco de la Casita** and at **Playa del Pozo**, cosie-optional bathers had discovered **Playa de la Arena** to be only a short hike from **Quemada**, and there was increasing interest from serious hikers in the **Femés - Papagayo - Playa Blanca** trek. With five walking routes published in Walk! Lanzarote, this previously empty landscape started to fill with walkers. The growing popularity of this wild landscape was noticed by the local authorities who decided to install a unique system of colour coded wayposts as their guide to people following the walking trails. Such an initiative is to be applauded even if the system of wayposts are completely different to the 'classic' system used by the *Cabildo* (island government) for the **La Geria** region.

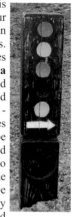

Unfortunately, the leaflet explaining the wayposted routes was not available from the tourist information offices we visited, it seems the leaflet ran out some time ago, so the only reference material are the 'Red de Senderos de Los Ajaches' notice boards at the entry points to the Hidden Barrancos. You could take a digital photo of the board and refer to this, but the map is rather 'freehand' and your image too small for accurate navigation or for establishing where you are, so we've superimposed the Los Ajaches routes as shown on the notice boards onto a section of our Lanzarote Tour & Trail Map, which gives more information and is more portable than a notice board, but is still subject to the freehand accuracy of the artist.

Seven walking routes are shown on notice boards and wayposts, which we interpret as:-

WHITE ROUTE Femés - Quemada is our Walk 19 Femés to Playa Quemada - The Missing Link.

PINK ROUTE Femés circular back to **Femés** is our Walk 16 The Hidden Barrancos; our first route in this region, originally published in 1995..

LILAC/PURPLE ROUTE Femés - Playa Quemada is a variation linking our Walk 16 and Walk 19 routes. Basically, follow Walk 16 to the path junction at waypoint 5, then take the path down into the **Barranco de la Higuera** to link with Walk 19 inland of **Playa del Pozo**, then Walk 19 to **Playa Quemada**.

BLACK ROUTE Playa Quemada - Casitas de Femés is part of Walk 19 (in reverse) until waypoint 6 where you turn off to walk up the **Barranco del Frailes**. At the top of the *barranco* you come onto a dirt track taking you into the hamlet of **Casita de Femés**.

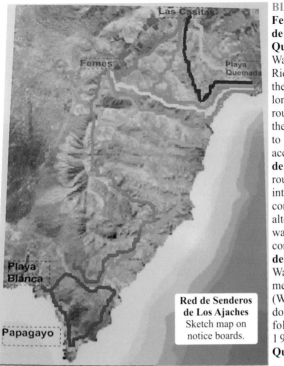

BLUE ROUTE
Femés - Casitas de Femés - Playa Quemada is our Walk 17 Femes Ridge, but taking the easier though longer alternative route (staying on the walking trail) to the dirt track accessing **Casita de Femés**. The route does not go into the hamlet, continuing on the alternative route walking trail to come into **Valle del Pozo**. Where Walk 17 (Wp.11) meets Walk 19 (Wp.4) we turn down the valley following Walk 19 to **Playa Quemada**.

Red de Senderos de Los Ajaches
Sketch map on notice boards.

RED ROUTE **Femés** - inland of **Playa Blanca East** is our Walk 18 Femés to Playa Blanca, following the dirt track all the way to waypoint 11 where the Red Route takes the main track inland, our Alt route, then turns right at the next main junction to finish on the dirt track T-junction inland of **Playa Mujeres**.

DEEP PURPLE ROUTE Circular route from **Playa Blanca East** to **Papagayo** and the eastern beaches before striking inland to join the Red Route, then turning left at the T-junction to meet its outward route at **Playa Mujeres**. This is a combination of our Walk 10 Papagayo Beach, then Walk 18 in reverse to **El Pasito** then inland to join the dirt tracks in the desert.

2nd BLUE ROUTE **Playa Quemada** - inland of **Playa Blanca East**. An interesting route initially following our Walk 20 Playa del Pozo route and then striking over the headland to head up the **Barranco de la Casita** before crossing the next ridge into the **Barranco de los Dises** to come down towards the coast before heading southwest to link up with our Walk 18 and the Red Route. Unfortunately our own and other people's GPS records of walking in this region do not confirm the route shown on the map board.

Our **Lanzarote Tour & Trail Super-Durable Map** (published 2012) provides a much more accurate picture of the walking trails in this region; the trails shown on our map are all prepared from gps ground survey records.

Personally, we would much prefer our Walk 18 route as a way of reaching

Papagayo and **Playa Blanca**, but this more coastal route does mean that you can walk from **Playa Quemada** to **Playa Blanca** by a relatively coastal route.

If you wish to take the direct route from **Playa Quemada** to **Papagayo/Playa Blanca** then we suggest that you follow the trails shown on the **Lanzarote Tour & Trail Super-Durable Map 3rd edition** (2012). Trying to translate that blue wiggly line on the map board into a walking route over this challenging terrain could end up as an exercise in frustration!

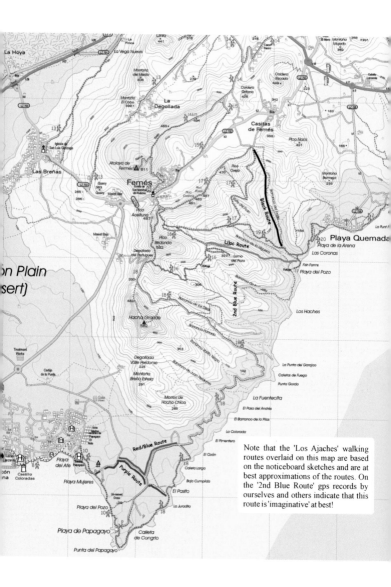

Note that the 'Los Ajaches' walking routes overlaid on this map are based on the noticeboard sketches and are at best approximations of the routes. On the '2nd Blue Route' gps records by ourselves and others indicate that this route is 'imaginative' at best!

Set on Lanzarote's western volcanic coastline, the little settlement of **El Golfo** is one of those 'must call in at' destinations if you have a hire car. Set 6km west of the **Yaiza** roundabout at the end of the LZ-704 minor road, the small settlement is a delightful place for a long lunch, morning coffee or afternoon tea, at one of the seafront restaurants overlooking the Atlantic Ocean breaking against lava rocks and black sand beaches. There are also some tourist 'knick-knack' shops and a mini market for self-caterers, plus a new tourist restaurant set on the entrance to this illogical village. 'Illogical' because there seems to be no historic reason why anybody would settle here - except that they have! **El Golfo** now exists to cater for the daily visitors to this delightful haven that's a full time shift away from the 'brassy' resorts.

El Golfo would be a delightful base for leisure walking, except that there didn't seem to be any suitable routes. Walk 24 has an optional finish here but our 'A Path Between Two Seas' is hardly leisurely. That was until we were finalising the design of the new book and map when a fanmail arrived from Neil Cameron, giving us an outline of a circular route he had completed using a path we didn't know about, along with the optional end of Walk 24. We've not walked the route ourselves but it sounds idyllic. After a relaxed breakfast, drive to **El Golfo** to complete the 7km circuit (good footwear essential along with water), so that when you arrive back you'll feel justified when indulging in a long lunch at one of the seafront restaurants.

Quoting from Neil:-

"There's a path well w a y m a r k e d (except the very northern part, where it can still be seen if you look carefully)

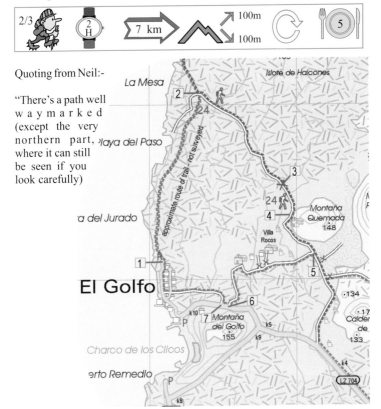

with little rocks running all the way from the north end of **El Golfo** to exactly opposite where your walk 24 coming south meets the dirt track to **Playa del Paso**.

The path leaving **El Golfo** is clear but quickly becomes almost totally rocky requiring careful footwork (I know, I tripped and skinned my hand!). The path (about 1 metre wide) is bordered by a row of stones on either side at many parts so is quite easy to follow, although occasionally you wonder where it will go next as it twists and turns, rising and falling.

The last section before reaching the track is hardest to follow, but not that difficult if you keep looking. We used this to have a nice circular walk starting and ending in **El Golfo**. The dirt track back into **El Golfo** is worth using as it avoids the road and there is a nice gravel path to the right of a ditch on the right hand (north) side of the track.".

Approximate timings:-
Wp.1 0M, Wp.2 25M, Wp.3 45M, Wp.4 50M, Wp.5 62M, Wp.6 85M, Wp.7 87M, Wp.1 107M

GLOSSARY

This glossary contains Spanish and Canarian words found in the text (shown in *italics*), plus other local words that you may encounter.

a

abandonado	abandoned
abierto	open
acantilado	cliff
agua	water
agua no potable	water (not drinkable)
agua potable	drinking water
aljibe	sunken water tank
alto	high
aparcamiento	parking
arepa/arepera	deep fried savoury snack/bar specialising in arepas
autopista	main road, motorway
ayuntamiento	town hall

b

bajo	low
barranco	ravine
bocadillo	bread roll
bodegón	inn
buceo	scuba diving

c

cabezo	peak, summit
cabra	goat
café	coffee
caldera	collapsed cone (volcanic area)
calima	suspended dust brought in by hot east winds
calle	street
camino	trail, path, track
camino	
particular	private road
camino real	old donkey trail (lit. royal road)
carne	meat
carretera	main road
casa	house
casa rural	country house accommodation to let
caserío	hamlet, village
castillo	castle
cementario	cemetery
centro comercial	shopping centre
cerrado	closed
cerveza (caña, presión, lata)	beer (small, large, *jarra*, draught, can)
charco	pool
choza	shelter
clinica	clinic, hospital
colmena	bee hive
comida	food
conquistador	conqueror
cordillera	mountain range
correos	post office
cortijo	farmstead
costa	coast
coto privado de caza	private hunting area
Cruz Roja	Red Cross (medical aid)
cuesta	slope
cueva	cave

cumbre	summit
d	
degollado	pass
derecha	right (direction)
desayuno	breakfast
desprendimiento	landslide
e	
ermita	chapel
Espacio Naturaleza Protegido	protected area of natural beauty
estación de autobus/ guagua	bus station
este	east
f	
farmacia	chemist
faro	lighthouse
fiesta	holiday, celebration
finca	farm, country house
g	
gasolinera	petrol station
gofio	flour made from roast maize, wheat or barley
guagua	bus
Guardia Civil	police
guia	guide
h	
hornito	lava bubble
hostal	hostel, accommodation
hoya	depression (geological)
huevos	eggs
i	
iglesia	church
información	information
isla	island
izquierda	left (direction)
j	
jameo	volcanic tube
jamón	ham
l	
libreria	bookshop
llano	plain
lluvioso	rainy
lomo	broad-backed ridge
m	
Majos/Mahos	Lazarote's original inhabitants
malpais	'bad lands' wild, barren countryside
malvasia	Malmsey grapes and wine
mapa	map
mareta	raised water collection tank
mariscos	shellfish
mercado	market
mirador	lookout/viewing point
mojo	spicy sauce based on olive oil, tomatoes and chilis
montaña	mountain
museo	museum
n	
norte	north
nublado	cloudy
o	
oeste	west
oficina de turismo	tourist office
p	
paella	rice dish, usually with seafood or meat
panadería	bakery
papas arrugadas	wrinkled potatoes (small potatoes in their skins cooked in salt water)
parapente	hang-glider
parque eólico	wind farm
pastelería	cake shop
peligro	danger
pensión	guesthouse
pescado	fish
pico	peak
picon	black volcanic rock/sand
pista	dirt road/track
pista (forestal)	forest road/track
playa	beach
plaza	square
policia	police
postre	dessert
potaje	thick soup
pozo	well
prohibido el paso	no entry
puente	bridge
puerto	port, mountain pass
q	
queso	cheese
r	
risco	cliff
roque	rock
ruta	route
s	
salida	exit
salinas	salt pans
sangria	wine with fruit punch served in a jug of ice
senda	path, track
sendero	foot path
sin salida	no through road/route
sirocco	hot, dust-laden wind from Africa
sur	south
t	
tapas	bar snacks
té	tea
tienda	shop
tipico	traditional bar/eating place
tormentoso	stormy
torre	tower
tuberia	water pipe
v	
valle	valley
vega	meadow
ventoso	windy
vino (blanco, tinto, rosado)	wine (white, red, rosé)
volcán	volcano
z	
zocos	crescent shaped vine enclosures (as seen in La Geria)
zona recreativa	recreation area
zumo/zumería	freshly pressed fruit juice/juice bar

CYCLING ON LANZAROTE

Lanzarote is a surprisingly varied island; you cycle up steep valleys through green palm trees and black *picon* fields, then head down from the ridge to the coast where the Atlantic bursts onto black lava-cliffs. In winter it's at its most interesting, full of colour as plant life bursts from the otherwise desert-like terrain. It's a great mountain biking destination, both on and off road and perfect for winter training; there's also the sports complex of Club La Santa open all year. Sporting competitions such as Lanzarote Ironman (in May each year) attract more and more participants.

For the mountain biker, Lanzarote can be divided into three regions; the north where you ride along the coast or through steep green valleys, either on quiet country roads or over rocky trails and single tracks; the centre of the island, less hilly - but far away from being flat, and the south which is again steep and very rocky, but less green. This section offers high mountain dirt tracks and gentle gradients along the coast or through lava fields.

- **What the cyclist will find only occasionally** - but usually can avoid - wet conditions.
- **What might surprise you** - going faster climbing up than rolling down - due to the wind.
- **What might amaze you** - stunning views all over the island.
- **What you have to see** - the landscape around Timanfaya National Park - unforgettable!

Other useful information:-

- In winter bring a windbreaker, maybe zip-on-sleeves and you'll need sun protection all year round.
- It's the law to wear a bike helmet on Lanzarote. One will be included in your cycle hire from all reputable rental companies on the island.
- Take your **Lanzarote Super-Durable Tour & Trail Map**
- When riding off-road please respect local signs and don't leave trails or pistes as this can damage the island's delicate ecosystems.
- Be alert to loose or abandoned dogs - they might view you as escaping goats.

If you need any further advice or want to join us on one of our guided rides don't hesitate to contact us via email:

bike@mylanzarote.com info@tommys-bikes.com
info@bikelanzarote.com

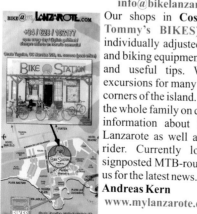

Our shops in **Costa Teguise** (Bike Station and Tommy's BIKES) stock all kind of bicycles individually adjusted to your needs. We carry spares and biking equipment and also offer guided excursions and useful tips. We've been running our bike excursions for many years and we know all the hidden corners of the island. Our team offers you easy rides for the whole family on quiet roads and trails, with loads of information about traditions and local history of Lanzarote as well as hardcore trails for the serious rider. Currently local authorities are designing signposted MTB-routes for Lanzarote - please contact us for the latest news.

Andreas Kern

www.mylanzarote.com   www.tommys-bikes.com

BUS TIMETABLES

- Bus times change; ask for the latest version on arrival. The Biosphere Information Office (almost faces you on emerging from Arrecife airport baggage hall) usually has free copies or ask in the Puerto del Carmen Information office (near the beach).
- Occasionally buses showing numbers other than that designated for the route will arrive at the stop; ask the driver if he is going to your destination.
- Don't rely on catching the last bus back; carry taxi phone numbers and a mobile phone, just in case. Most villages have a public phone, otherwise, try a bar.
- Bono bus tickets can be purchased for €12 and €22 on buses and offer a 30% discount off the standard fare.
- For current information visit: **www.arrecifebus.es**

N.B. Some services run from early morning to late at night to the early hours. Here we've selected those times most likely to be useful for getting to and from walking routes during daylight hours.

01 ARRECIFE - COSTA TEGUISE - ARRECIFE
Playa de Reducto - Juzgados - Bus Station - Los Alonso - Los Mármoles - Las Caletas (Costa Teguise) - Hotel Oasis - Playa Roca - Playa Bastián - Pueblo Marinero - Lanzarote Gardens - Hotel Salinas
MONDAY TO FRIDAY (excluding holidays)
From Arrecife Bus Station to Costa Teguise: approx every 20 mins from 06:40 until 22:40
From Costa Teguise to Arrecife: approx every 20 mins until 07:00 to 22.40
SATURDAY, SUNDAY & HOLIDAYS
From Arrecife Bus Station to Costa Teguise: approx every 30 mins from 06:40 until 23:10
From Costa Teguise to Arrecife: approx very 30 mins from 07:00 until 23:00

02 ARRECIFE - PUERTO DEL CARMEN
Bus Station - Rotonda S Fco Javier/Juzgados on return journey - Playa del Reducto - Poligono Playa Honda - Matagorda - Hotel Jameos - Costa Mar - Hotel San Antonio - C C Welcome See - La Peñita - C C Arena Dorada - Apart. Los Fariones - C C Biosfera - Balcón del Mar
MONDAY TO FRIDAY (excluding holidays)
From Bus Station to Puerto del Carmen: approx every 20 mins from 06:20 until 22:20
From Puerto del Carmen to Bus Station: approx every 20 mins from 07:00 until 22:20
SATURDAY, SUNDAY & HOLIDAYS
From Bus Station to Puerto del Carmen: approx every 30 mins from 07:20 until 22:20
From Puerto del Carmen to Bus Station: approx every 30 mins from 08:00 until 22:30

03 COSTA TEGUISE - PUERTO DEL CARMEN
Hotel Salinas (Costa Teguise) - Lanzarote Gardens - Pueblo Marinero - Playa Bastián - Playa Roca - Hotel Oasis - Las Caletas - Los Alonso - Arrecife Bus Station - Playa del Reducto - Poligono P Honda Matagorda - Costa Mar - Hotel San Antonio - La Peñita - Apart Los Fariones - C C Biosfera - Balcón del Mar
MONDAY TO FRIDAY (excluding holidays)
From Costa Teguise to Puerto del Carmen: approx every 20 mins from 07:00 until 21:20
From Puerto del Carmen to Costa Teguise: approx every 20 mins from 07:00 until 21.40
SATURDAY, SUNDAY & HOLIDAYS
From Costa Teguise to Puerto del Carmen: approx every 30 mins from 09:00 until 22.00
From Puerto del Carmen to Costa Teguise: approx every 30 mins from 10:00 until 21.00

05 ARRECIFE - FEMÉS
Arrecife Bus Station - Rotonda S Fco Javier - Playa del Reducto - Poligono P Honda - Tías centre - Los Lirios - Iglesia de Conil - Conil centre - Palmera Asomada - La Asomada centre - Mácher Petrol Station - Palmera de Mácher - Puerto Calero crossroads - Las Casitas - El Puente de Femés - Femés church
MONDAY TO FRIDAY only (excluding holidays)
From Arrecife Bus Station: 08:15 14:00 19:15
From Femés: 09:00 14.45 20:00

07 ARRECIFE - MÁGUEZ
Arrecife Bus Station - Altavista - Cuesta del Gallo (Tahiche) - César Manrique crossroads - Tahiche - Las Cabreras - Nazaret - Teguise town hall (ayuntamiento) - Teguise church - El Mojón crossroads - Plaza de Guatiza - Jardín de Cactus - Mala correos - Mala de Abajo - Tabayesco - Los Morros - Punta Mujeres - Bar Palenque - La Plaza, Haría - La Cruz, Haría - La Molina de Máguez - Sociedad de Maguez
MONDAY TO FRIDAY (excluding holidays)
From Arrecife Bus Station to Máguez: 08:00 10:00 12:30 14:30 16.30 18:30 20:30
From Máguez to Arrecife Bus Station: 07:00 09:00 11:00 13:30 15:30 17:30 19.30
SATURDAYS, SUNDAY AND HOLIDAYS
From Arrecife Bus Station to Máguez: 08:00 10.00 12.00 14.00 18.00 20.00
From Máguez to Arrecife Bus Station: 07:00 09.00 11.00 13.00 19.00 20:45

09 ARRECIFE - ÓRZOLA
Arrecife Bus Station - Altavista - Cuesta de Gallo (Tahiche) - César Manrique crossroads - Tahiche - Las Cabreras - Nazaret - Teguise town hall (ayuntamiento) - Teguise church - Teseguite de Abajo - El Mojón crossroads - Plaza de Guatiza - Jardín de Cactus - Mala post office (correos) - Mala de Abajo - Tabayesco

- Arrieta - Los Morros - Punta Mujeres - Bar Palenque - El Callao - Órzola muelle
MONDAY TO FRIDAY (excluding holidays)
From Arrecife Bus Station: 07:40 10:30 12.00 15:30 17.00
From Órzola: 08:30 11:30 13.10 16:40 18.10
SATURDAY, SUNDAY AND HOLIDAYS
From Arrecife Bus Station: 07:40 15:30 17.00
From Órzola: 08:30 16:40 18.10
10 ARRECIFE - LOS VALLES
Arrecife Bus Station - Altavista - Cuesta de Gallo (Tahiche) - El Jamonal - César Manrique crossroads - Tahiche - Las Cabreras - Nazaret - Teguise town hall (ayuntamiento) - Centro de Salud de Teguise - Teguise church - Teseguíte de Abajo - El Mojón - Sociedad de Los Valles - Valle Arriba
MONDAY TO FRIDAY only (excluding holidays)
From Arrecife Bus Station: 06.30 10:00 14:00 16:00 20.40
From Los Valles: 07:00 10:30 14:30 16:30 21.10
11 COSTA TEGUISE - TEGUISE MARKET
Hotel Salinas - Lanzarote Gardens - Pueblo Marinero - Playa Bastián - Playa Roca - Hotel Oasis - Market
SUNDAY only
From Costa Teguise: 09:00 09:30 10:00 10:30 11:00
From Teguise market: 12:00 12:30 13:00 13:15 14:00
12 PUERTO DEL CARMEN - TEGUISE MARKET
Balcón del Mar - Las Vistas - Apart Los Fariones - C C Arena Dorada - La Peñita - C C Welcome See - Hotel San Antonio - Costa Mar - Hotel Jameos - Matagorda - Teguise market
SUNDAY only
From Puerto del Carmen to Teguise market: 09:00 09:30 10:00 10:30 11:00
From Teguise market to Puerto del Carmen: 12:00 12:30 13:00 13:15 14:00
13 PLAYA BLANCA - TEGUISE MARKET
Playa Blanca port (muelle) - Playa Blanca Bus Station - Rotonda La Hoya - Aljibe de Yaiza - Yaiza Supermarket - Uga church - Puerto Calero crossroads - Palmera de Mácher - Mácher petrol station - La Finca de Mácher - Balcón del Mar - C C Biosfera - Football ground - Los Lirios - Tías centre - Ferretería de Tías - Poligono Playa Honda - Playa del Reducto - Juzgados - Arrecife bus station - Teguise market
SUNDAY only
From Playa Blanca to Teguise market: 09:10
From Teguise market to Playa Blanca: 13:00
16 ARRECIFE - LA SANTA
Arrecife Bus Station - General Hospital - Avda de las Palmeras, San Bartolomé - San Bartolomé crossroads - Mozaga post office (correos) - La Caseta de Tao - La Tienda de Tiagua - La Vegueta post office (correos) - Curva La Vegueta - Las Cadenas - Los Dolores - Mancha Blanca - Guigua (Tinajo) - Tajaste - El Calvario - La Plaza de Tinajo - La Cañada - El Cuchillo - La Santa - La Santa Sport
MONDAY TO FRIDAY (excluding holidays)
From Arrecife Bus Station to La Santa: approx hourly from 07.00 until 19.00
From La Santa to Arrecife Bus Station: approx hourly from 07.00 until 19.00
SATURDAYS, SUNDAYS AND HOLIDAYS
From Arrecife Bus Station to La Santa: 08:00 10:15 12:00 14.00 15.45 17.30 19.00 20.30
From La Santa to Arrecife Bus Station: 07:00 08:45 11.00 12.45 14.45 16.45 18.15 19.45
19 ARRECIFE - LA ASOMADA
Arrecife Bus Station - Rto S Fco Javier - Playa del Reducto - Poligonon Playa Honda - Ferretería de Tías - Tías centre - Los Lirios - Conil church - Conil centre - Palmera Asomada - La Asomada centre - Mácher petrol station - Palmera de Mácher - Puerto Calero crossroads
MONDAY TO FRIDAY only (excluding holidays)
From Arrecife Bus Station: 07:00 08:15 14:00 19:15
From La Asomada: 07:30 09:20 15.05 20:20
20 ARRECIFE - CALETA FAMARA
Arrecife Bus Station - General Hospital - Avda Las Palmeras (San Bartolomé) - San Bartolomé crossroads - Mozaga post office (correos) - La Caseta de Tao - La Tienda de Tiagua - Sociedad de Muñique - Soo - Caleta Famara
MONDAY TO FRIDAY only (excluding holidays)
From Arrecife Bus Station to Caleta Famara: 06:30 09:45 14.00 17:45 20:45
From Caleta Famara to Arrecife Bus Station: 07:00 10:30 14:45 18:30 21:30
21 ARRECIFE - PLAYA HONDA
OUTWARD JOURNEY Arrecife Bus Station - Registro - Rotonda S Fco Javier - Playa del Reducto - Poligono Playa Honda - Calle Mayor, Playa Honda - Instituto Playa Honda
INWARD JOURNEY Calle San Borondón, Playa Honda - Princess Ico - Rotonda Playa Reducto - Gran Hotel - Casino - Parque Viejo - Escuela de Pesca - Policia Nacional - Los Alonso - Arrecife Bus Station
MONDAY TO FRIDAY only (excluding holidays)
From Arrecife Bus Station to Playa Honda: approx every 15-30 mins from 08.10 until 22:10
From Playa Honda to Arrecife Bus Station: approx every 15-30 mins from 08.25 until 23.05
22 ARRECIFE - AIRPORT

OUTWARD JOURNEY Arrecife Bus Station - Registro - Rotonda S Fco Javier - Playa del Reducto - Poligono Playa Honda - Airport terminal 1 - Airport terminal 2

INWARD JOURNEY Airport terminal 2 - Esq Calle Mástil, Playa Honda - Deiland, Playa Honda - Playa del Reducto - Juzgados - Arrecife Bus Station

MONDAY TO FRIDAY only (excluding holidays)

Arrecife Bus Station to Airport: approx every 25 mins from 07.55 until 22.30

Airport to Arrecife Bus Station: approx every 25 mins from 07.00 until 22.15

23 ARRECIFE - PLAYA HONDA - AIRPORT

OUTWARD JOURNEY Arrecife Bus Station - Registro - Rotonda S Fco Javier - Playa del Reducto - Poligono Playa Honda - Airport terminal 1 - Airport terminal 2

INWARD JOURNEY Airport terminal 2 - Esq Calle Mástil, Playa Honda - Calle Mayor, Playa Honda - Calle San Borondón - Princesa Ico - Rotonda Playa Reducto - Gran Hotel - Casino - Parque Viejo - Escuela de Pesca - Policia Nacional - Los Alonso - Arrecife Bus Station

SATURDAY, SUNDAY AND HOLIDAYS only

From Bus Station to Airport: approx every 50 mins from 07.00 until 21.00

From Airport to Arrecife Bus Station: approx every 50 mins from 07.10 until 20.20

24 ARRECIFE - PUERTO CALERO

OUTWARD JOURNEY Los Alonso - Arrecife Bus Station - Rotonda s Fco Javier - Playa del Reducto - Poligono Playa Honda - Matagorda (Puerto del Carmen) - Hotel Jameos - Costa Mar - Hotel San Antonio - CC Welcome See - La Peñita - C C Arena Dorada - Apart Los Fariones - C C Biosfera - Balcón del Mar - Puerto Calero

MONDAY TO FRIDAY only (excluding holidays)

From Alonso, Arrecife to Puerto Calero: 07:00 09:00 11:20 15:00 19:40 23:20

From Puerto Calero to Alonso, Arrecife: 07:30 09:30 11:50 15:30 20:10 24:00

SATURDAY, SUNDAY & HOLIDAYS

From Alonso, Arrecife to Puerto Calero: 07:20 10:20 11:50 14:50 19:50 23:20

From Puerto Calero to Alonso, Arrecife: 07:50 10:50 12:20 15:20 20:20 24:00

26 ARRECIFE - YÉ

Arrecife Bus Station - Altavista - Cuesta del Gallo/Tahiche - El Jamonal - Cesar Manrique crossroads - Tahiche - Las Cabreras - Nazaret - Teguise town hall (ayuntamiento) - Centro Salud de Teguise - Teseguite church - Teseguite de Abajo - El Mojón crossroads - Plaza de Guatiza - Cactus Garden - Mala de Abajo - Tabayesco - Arrieta - Los Morros - Punta Mujeres - Bar Palenque, Punta Mujeres - Calle San Juan, Haría - La Plaza, Haría - La Cruz, Haría - La Molina de Máguez - Sociedad de Máguez - Guinate crossroads - Yé

MONDAY TO FRIDAY only (excluding holidays)

From Arrecife Bus Station to Yé: 18:00

From Yé to Arrecife Bus Station: 06:50

30 PLAYA BLANCA CIRCULAR

Itinerary 1

Playa Blanca Bus Staion - Sun Beach - C C Papagayo - Princesa Yaiza - Castillo del Aguila - Ciudad Jardin 2 - San Marcial 2 - Las Coloradas - San Marcial 1 - Marina Rubicón - Playa Dorada - Lanzarote Princess - Playa Blanca port) - Flamingo - Volcanes 2 - Volcanes 1 - Natura Palace - Rubicón Palace - La Goleta 2 - Faro Park - Los Arcos - Bajo Los Riscos - Jardin del Sol - Virginia Park - El Pueblito - Collegio - La Perla 1 - Las Margaritas - Playa Limones - Casas del Sol - Playa Blanca Bus Station

DAILY SERVICE

approx every 30 mins from 06.30 until 22.00

60 ARRECIFE - PLAYA BLANCA

Arrecife Bus Station - Rto S Fco Javier - Playa del Reducto - Poligonon Playa Honda - Ferretería de Tías - Tías centre - C C Biosfera, Pto del Carmen - Balcón del Mar - La Finca de Mácher - Mácher petrol station - Palmera de Mácher - Puerto Calero crossroads - Uga church - Aljibe de Yaiza - Centro de Salud de Yaiza - Rotónda La Hoya - - Las Breñas 123 - Playa Blanca Bus Station - Playa Blanca port (muelle)

MONDAY TO FRIDAY only (excluding holidays)

From Arrecife Bus Station to Playa Blanca: approx hourly from 07.00 until 21.00

From Playa Blanca to Arrecife Bus Station: approx hourly from 08.00 until 22.00

SATURDAY, SUNDAY & HOLIDAYS

From Arrecife Bus Station to Playa Blanca: approx two hourly from 07.00 until 21.00

From Playa Blanca to Arrecife Bus Station: approx two hourly from 08.00 until 22.00

61 PUERTO DEL CARMEN - PLAYA BLANCA (N.B. this route commences from Arrecife Bus Station approximately 30 mins before arriving in Puerto del Carmen)

C C Biosfera - Balcón del Mar - La Finca de Mácher - Mácher Petrol Station - Palmera de Mácher - Puerto Calero crossroads - Uga church - Yaiza supermarket - Aljibe de Yaiza - Centro de Salud de Yaiza - Rotonda La Hoya - Playa Blanca Bus Station - Playa Blanca port (muelle)

MONDAY TO FRIDAY (excluding holidays)

From Puerto del Carmen to Playa Blanca: approx hourly from 09.35 until 21.35

From Playa Blanca to Puerto del Carmen: approx hourly from 08:30 until 22.20

SATURDAY, SUNDAY AND HOLIDAYS

From Puerto del Carmen to Playa Blanca: approx every two hours from 10:05 until 20.05

From Playa Blanca to Puerto del Carmen: approx every two hours from 09.00 until 21.00